MARY MARY QUITE

On Raising Children (And Other Mind-Altering Substances)

MARY HUCKSTEP
Illustrated by DAVID CONDRY

Busy Bee Publishing • Fountain Valley, California

Published by Busy Bee Publishing
Fountain Valley, California
www.marymaryquite.com

First U.S. Book Edition: September, 2014

ISBN: 978-0-9907071-0-3

Library of Congress Control Number: 2014915124

Also available in digital form on: Kindle and Audible

Printed in the United States of America

Dedications

To Mom and Old Hunk, my biggest fans and loyal cheerleaders. And to all my kids, grandkids, in-laws and outlaws. I couldn't have done it without you, and I wouldn't want to try. Thanks for all the fun, ya'all! I love you more than popcorn. SWAK!
Mary, Mom, G-ma

To two lovely ladies: my wife and my one-year-old daughter, my most trusted creative consultant and my most exuberant front-row audience member, respectively. And to an ever-growing family of fellow artists, teachers, thinkers, and pioneers. Thank you.
D.J.C.

Table of Contents

1
MMQ:
On Valentine's Day

Good old Hunk proposed on Valentine's Day. Finally!

I'd been trying to hook him for months, luring him to see the merits of matrimony, but he hadn't even nibbled at the bait.

I was beginning to think I'd never land him.

Two weeks before Valentine's Day, I burst into tears.

"What's wrong?" he asked.

I poured out my heart to him (big mistake) and explained that I'd had a problem for months. And since he was my best friend, I'd wanted to talk to him about my problem . . . but actually, I couldn't talk to him because, in fact, he *was* the problem.

(This did seem logical at the time.)

I was ready to pledge my love forever – before God and witnesses – but I knew that he was not. Ten months of weekly dating and nightly phone calls had won my heart, but he was still deliberating.

I had to admit, "Guilty as charged!"

But he kept crying, "Innocent!"

I pushed for a lifetime sentence.

He favored probation.

Between the two of us, we had a hung jury. And I had been going insane.

After I explained my problem, I saw the light of understanding dawn in my sweetheart's eyes . . . followed by something that strikes terror into the heart of any woman: Fear in the eyes of her man. Primordial fear.

It was the panic of the stampeding antelope, moments before the lioness lunges at his neck and wrestles him to his doom. I recognized fear as my enemy and backed off. Way off.

I decided to try a different approach.

I went shopping!

I purchased enough Valentine cards to open my own Hallmark store, then went to work, sending two and sometimes three a day – every day for two weeks – right up until Valentine's Day.

They weren't sticky and sweet. Oh, no. They were peppy and fun, and I covered each one with jokes and pictures – just the kind of glittering, spinning lures I needed to hook my big fish.

I cast each one in the letter box, then reeled it back in two days later, by phone. "Here fishy, fishy. Better things over here! Follow the lures!"

Strike!

I knew he was about to swallow the bait when he picked me up for dinner February 14th sporting a suit, a tie, and a new haircut. We drove for an hour to a fancy restaurant, where we waited another hour for a table which never materialized, despite reservations.

So we left and found a place nearby, called "Harpoon Henry's," a restaurant complete

Ah, the romantic moment.

with whaling décor and "The Catch of the Day." (Hmmmmm!) Here, we'd have to wait only ten minutes. Great!

We headed for the lounge where, over drinks, my guy finally popped the question . . . well, sorta.

"I think we should talk about marriage," he said, then grabbed a handful of peanuts and stuffed them into his mouth. (Ah, the romantic moment.)

I managed to say something nonchalant like, "Oh . . . okay, if you think so." But that was it!

In an instant, I had been transformed from an intelligent woman into a drooling, leering, imbecile. I had been sipping something green, and I began feeling progressively greener. My cheeks were growing warm. Casually, I wondered if they might be turning green.

By the time we were seated and had ordered dinner, I was in a complete state of shock and the entire room looked green.

When our dinners arrived, my guy continued chatting about married life, and did I think we should open up one IRA or two?

First, he ate his dinner. Then, he ate mine. (I can tell you from firsthand experience that imbeciles do not have appetites.) I know I spoke and it must have been in English – whatever I said – but all I can recall is staring at that huge iron harpoon that decorated the wall behind my big fish. It was situated just above his head, and I studied it as he chatted away.

"This is it," I kept thinking. "I've hooked my man and I've set the hook. But gee, that harpoon looks deadly."

(Does Cupid use harpoons sometimes?)

Cupid, please don't hurt him!

That was decades ago, back when old Hunk had hair, and I had a waistline. He had a bank account, and I had children in elementary school.

(It seemed like a good match.)

Now, I love my guy even more than when I married him. Now, even his faults are dear to me, simply because they are part and parcel of what makes him who he is. True, like other members of the human race, old Hunk can be a dirty rat sometimes. But he's my dirty rat, and I love him.

He wasn't just the catch of the day . . . he was the catch of a lifetime!

2
MMQ: On Raising Children

He looked like a miniature sled dog, with that white leather harness strapped around his chest and that white leather guideline clipped onto his back. His winter coat, made out of fuzzy fake fur, only added to the illusion.

But in some ways, he also looked like a wind-up toy, with his little legs carrying him unsteadily across turf and terrain in search of . . . well, whatever my two-year-old son happened to be in search of at that particular moment.

You know – chasing stray cats into oncoming traffic, following fire fighters into burning buildings, scurrying under parked cars in pursuit of tasty pill bugs, or charging into any-and-every open door, gate, garage, manhole, rat hole, or hell hole in sight.

Just the usual, death-defying, toddler stuff.

But I know one thing for sure, and that is this: Keeping Rascal on a leash (yes, that really is his name) saved more than his life. It also saved mine.

Now, before this darling boy had come into the world, I was no fan of the leashing of children. Seeing the occasional child on a leash elicited a whole host of negative, superior thoughts in my mind, most of which I kept to myself, despite my tsk-tsking noises and my back-piercing stare.

(You see, children who require leashes travel faster than a speeding Nerf dart, so their parents have to sprint after them as if they were training a greyhound for the races. Hence, my inevitable view of the guilty parent's back as he or she went racing by me, and my accompanying back-piercing stare.)

What kind of cruel, heartless, controlling person would treat a child like an animal? Had they no shame? Couldn't they confine their leash-keeping activities to behind closed doors? And where was the SPCA in such matters? (Or was it CBS? Or maybe it was NBC, or perhaps CPS?)

Never mind! They knew who they were, and they were contributing to the canine-control of children. The nerve of some people, to allow thousands of innocent children to be treated no better than a Labrador.

They'll be making them lap up puppy chow from a bowl, next.

And then came Rascal, my very own speeding Nerf dart. That little baby boy who, six months into gestation, kept me up nights – for three months straight – playing soccer ball with my kidneys and scoring goals on my rib cage. My darling baby boy, who at one hour old was doing push-ups in his bassinette – I kid you not.

That was an omen of things to come, and I should have realized what I was in for, right then and there.

But the real problem was that up until then, Rascal's older brother Sonny had always been a model child, all twenty months of his little life. So Sonny had

succeeded in lulling me into a kind of a motherly stupor, in which I couldn't even imagine a child of mine ever having a will of his own.

I baked a lot in those days and when the saintly Sonny was learning to crawl, I took him to the oven, pointed at the oven door and said, "This is very, very hot. If you touch it, it will hurt you and you will cry. So stay away and do not touch."

Sonny looked at me, looked at the oven, nodded as if to say, "Got it, Mom!" and then scooted away in complete obeisance to the oven god, who most certainly could hurt him and could make him cry. Yep, Sonny was an obedient child and I was a wonderful mother.

And then came Rascal. When Rascal learned to crawl, I took him to the oven and gave him the same spiel that I had given his saintly brother. Rascal's reaction? He looked at me, looked at the oven, narrowed his eyes as if to say, "Oh, yeah?" then shot his hand out and smacked the oven door.

"YOWWWW!" He yelped like a coyote at the pain. And instantly, I was transformed into the monster of all mothers.

I was raising a horrible, burn-scarred child, and life as I had known it was over.

Which leads me to one of my favorite sayings –

Want a guilt trip? Try being a parent.

And then there's the wonderful experience of choking down your own judgmental words and wading through a neck-deep puddle of humility – to clip a harness onto your young pup's back, so you can bring him to heel.

Instant guilt trip.

It has been a huge learning curve for me, to raise a strong-willed child. This mammoth assignment requires the battle tactics of a field marshal, the intimidation skills of an NFL linebacker, and the iron

will of a prison warden.

(All housed within a loving maternal heart, of course.)

Flash forward to Rascal's twelfth year on the planet, and the last time I faced off with the darling child. One Friday night, he had plans to go to Grandma and Grandpa's house to eat ice cream, play cards, and get a good spoiling, which was his grandparents' solemn duty to perform. But ten minutes before it was time to leave for G-ma and G-pa's, Rascal's friend, Wholly Terror, phoned and asked Rascal over for a sleepover.

And he wanted to go.

"Mom, can I spend the night at Wholly's house?"

"No, you don't cancel the plans you have with one person, just because a better offer comes along from someone else. You're going to G-ma and G-pa's house, as planned."

Have you ever seen a two-year-old throw a *bonafide* temper tantrum? With weeping and wailing and gnashing of teeth? Well, if you add in slamming doors and a Little League pitcher hurling laundry in all directions, you've just about got Rascal's reaction captured on video.

It was shocking. It was loud. And it was out of control.

But when, finally, he threw himself on the floor and started crying, I seized my chance. Well actually, I seized his ankles – both of them. And then I dragged him to the car, stuffed him into the passenger's seat, corralled him with the seatbelt, drove over to G-ma and G-pa's house, and dumped him on their driveway.

"He'll snap out of it," I answered their bewildered looks. (In a lifetime, or two, I heard myself thinking.)

Which leads me to yet another one of my pet sayings, one which my kids have heard approximately 7,398,463 times, all tolled. Ready?

Drum roll, please!

"Mom always wins."

KEEP CHILD ON LEASH

SEWER

What kind of cruel, heartless, controlling person
would treat a child like an animal?

"Mom is accountable to God and to society at large for how you turn out. And that's why Mom *has* to win."

Flash forward one year from the ankle-dragging incident, when thirteen-year-old Rascal won the coveted Dove award for the athlete with the best attitude and sportsman-like conduct in eighth grade – and I rest my case. Society at large had actually put their stamp of approval on our wild child.

(Nevermind that I should have received that Dove, and not him.)

(And no, that was not complaining – that was simply stating the obvious.)

(And yes, I did realize that the award was for good sportsmanship, and I was not necessarily modelling that trait right then. But I didn't feel particularly sporting at the time, okay?)

I was dumbfounded. Were they sure they had the right kid?

Rascal? Our hardcore, out-of-control kid?

Wow. It took some time for the shock to wear off, but eventually it did.

Rascal was gonna be okay.

I was gonna be okay!

So when I say that putting Rascal on a leash, way back when he was a toddler, not only saved his life but also mine, I can explain . . . in just one more story.

One day when I was taking Rascal for a walk (or rather, he was taking me), we dashed by an elderly lady, who, when she spied Rascal's leash, grabbed my arm and unleashed a beastly barrage of her own. What in blazes did I think I was doing? Was I completely heartless? How could a decent mother ever do such a thing to her child?

Well, I had been thinking about those very questions myself, for months, and I'd been waiting for someone to ask me just one of them. And here, this lady hit on all three!

"Lady," I told her, "I don't have

my son on a leash. He's the one who's in charge here, and it is he who has put me on a leash."

(Arf!)

And it was true. That little tyrant kept me in line for decades. I really had to clean up my act to raise that kid. No more wishy-washy thinking. And no more indecisiveness.

Because I was tethered to that child for the first eighteen years of his life, I actually became a more disciplined person, a person who got her act together for a lifetime.

Well, all that – and a few guilt trips thrown into the mix.

(Naturally.)

Which leads me to an oft-quoted scripture and my own personal take on some familiar words: "Raise up a child in the way that he should go, and when he is old . . . you will be exhausted."

3
MMQ:
On The Wife Store

Back in the days when I taught high school, I conversed with a fellow English teacher one day. The exchange went something like this –

I said, "That orange-flavored, Echinacea-and-goldenseal cough drop you gave me yesterday really helped my throat. Thanks for letting me try one. Where'd you get them?"

"I don't know," he answered.

"My wife bought them."

"Oh, I'll bet she got them at the wife store."

"Huh? Where's the wife store?"

Where's the wife store? Oh, I can explain.

The wife store is the place where wives go to buy things.

Is that clear? (Come to think of it, it's a bit more complicated than that.)

You see, there are many wife

stores. In fact, there are several versions of the wife store. Actually, every wife finds her own stores, but the locations vary from day to day.

Now, how do wives find these stores? Oh, we manage. For starters, their addresses are compiled and published annually in the national wife catalog, printed and distributed by the Wife Central Headquarters in Upper Saint Wifewood, Bring-Me-Home, Shopper-State, USA, 54321. Charge it!

So that helps.

Confused? Let me illustrate.

First, many of us shop at the "Swallow this because it's good for you" store. Never mind that the pellet we've just placed in your palm is green, and dotted with purple and brown specks, and tastes like motor oil. We went to a lot of trouble to buy this for you, so you'd better make us happy and swallow the ugly little thing.

Then there's the "I bought this on clearance, marked down from last month's sale, less my 20% coupon, so that Simon can grow into it by next summer" store. This store is modeled after the Scottish city of Brigadoon, which legend tells us becomes accessible to American tourists only once every 100 years. However, this particular wife store appears once every 30 days, usually on the first Friday after payday.

And then of course every wife knows about the "I haven't got a clue what we'll use this for but I had this hunch, so Sally and I went garage-saling and it caught my eye, save-you-lots" store. We place these items on the coffee table and call them conversation starters.

The wife store is the place where women flock to when their hubbies dunk their thumbs in Krazy Glue, then hunker down on the remote control for an intimate little eight hours with ESPN. Usually, there are no husbands allowed in wife stores. But then, which male in his right brain would want to enter?

(Besides, everyone knows that men prefer their left brains, anyway.)

It is common knowledge among more-experienced wives that husbands just cause confusion when, by chance or design, they stumble upon a wife store, themselves. I learned this lesson the hard way.

One Saturday morning near Christmas, I was too busy to go shopping, so I sent old Hunk to one of my favorite wife stores. I tried to make it easy for him. I really did. All I needed were some replacement gourmet spices from the "My, isn't this tasty, let's have this again" store.

On a piece of notebook paper, I listed all the names of the spices, exactly as they appeared on each one of the bottles. Then I placed all of the empty bottles in a plastic bag so old Hunk could match them up at the store. I drew him a map detailing exactly how to get there, gave him some money, told him he was a good

man and kissed him, then sent him out the door.

Three hours later, he returned triumphant.

Funny, I didn't know there was a Scratch and Dent Warehouse near the "My, isn't this tasty" store. And I certainly didn't recall having asked for a reversible drill, a post-hole digger, and six buckets of roof tar.

But he claimed that the "My isn't this tasty" store must have moved, because he'd driven up and down the street where I told him it was, three times, and he still couldn't find it.

I did some quick thinking, checked my mental map, then realized what had happened.

Old Hunk had driven straight to East Whatsit Way since he'd known exactly where that was, and he hadn't even looked at my directions. If he had looked at them, then he would have seen that I'd told him to go to West Whatsit Way, which is four miles on the other side of the Scratch

Three hours later, he returned triumphant.

and Dent Warehouse.

Pity. We could have had a delectable Indian curry that night when Hal and Joanie came over for dinner. As it was, we dined out – down the freeway at my favorite little French restaurant where they serve this great onion soup in heated bowls.

It's right next door to the "Buy this sweater for Auntie Margaret and save it in the back of your closet for Christmas, unless she gains weight or dyes her hair blonde, in which case it'll look just darling on you" store.

Joanie knew exactly where it was.

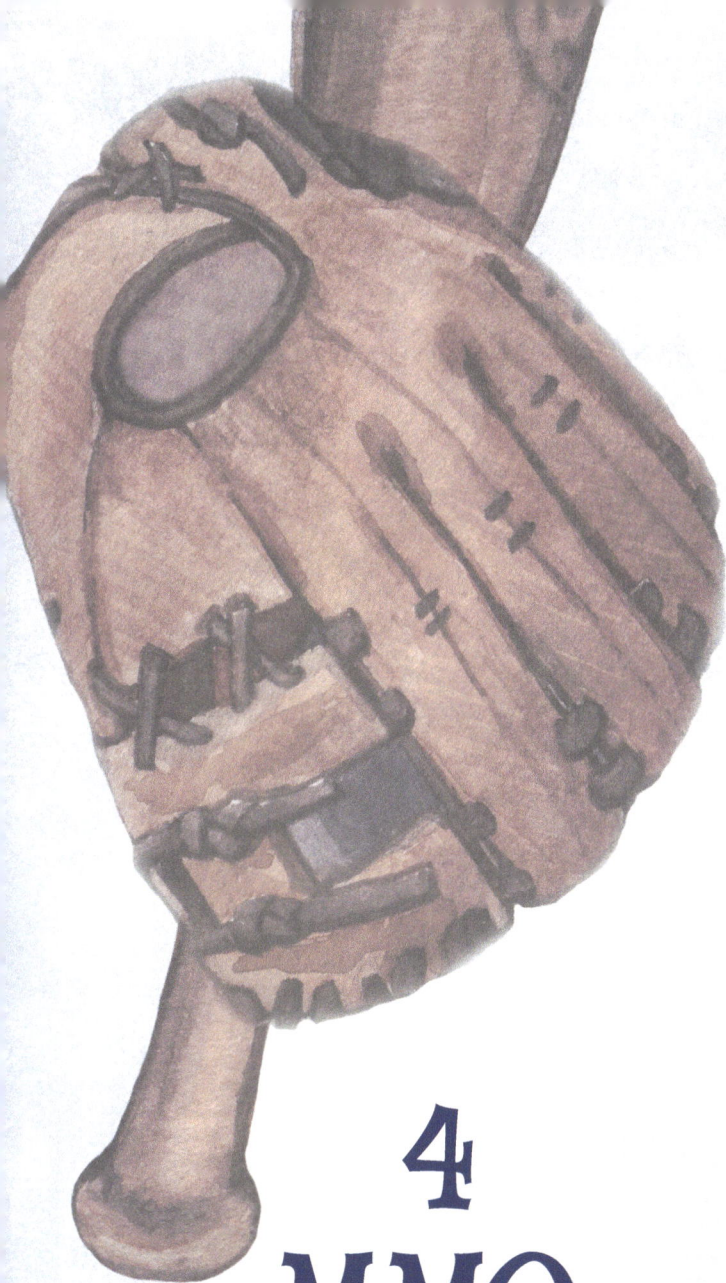

4
MMQ: On Springtime

Ah, spring! When blossoms cover the orchard and birds sing sweetly in the trees. Spring! When all of creation teems with life, and a young man's head fills with thoughts of . . . baseball?

No – not baseball. Tee ball, actually. You know that branch of Little League for the little guys, those who make up in heart for what they lack in skills? It's the freckle-face gang – the five and six-year-old baseball wannabes.

Tee ball. Where it takes fierce concentration and twenty swipes with a bat to tip a soft-core baseball off a stationary tee. Where every kid gets to play and nobody loses. And kids keep score by how many balls they can catch, not drop.

It's kid heaven, where adults become angels who speak nothing but praise. Every game and every practice, grown-ups behave like they're supposed to and kids never fail. These are the rules, and for some magical reason, everybody obeys them.

On the first day of practice, I picked up our little guy from the babysitter's early, allowing fifteen minutes to drive to the field two miles away. But – silly me – I hadn't allowed for a kid surprise. (After years of parenting, you'd think I would've learned, wouldn't you?)

"Uh, oh! I've got a hole in my sweatpants and you can see my underwear," ole Freckle Face greeted me and showed me his rear when I came through the door. (And boy did he, and boy could you!)

We drove straight home, where, with all the finesse of Laurel and Hardy, we re-clothed the wannabe as fast as we could. First we tried a short cut.

(Not good.) We tried to pull his sweatpants off over his shoes. (Okay, we knew that wouldn't work, now didn't we?)

So then we untied the double knot that keeps his hi-tops from falling off, loosened the laces, pulled back the tongue, yanked off the shoes (ooff!), dumped sand on the carpet, pulled off the holey sweatpants and denuded his feet of damp, sandy socks in the process.

Then we fished non-holey sweatpants and clean socks out of his bureau, slid the sweatpants up to his belly-button, maneuvered chubby feet into fresh socks, shoved his hi-tops back on, pushed the tongue back in, pulled the laces tight and re-doubled-knotted them, answered

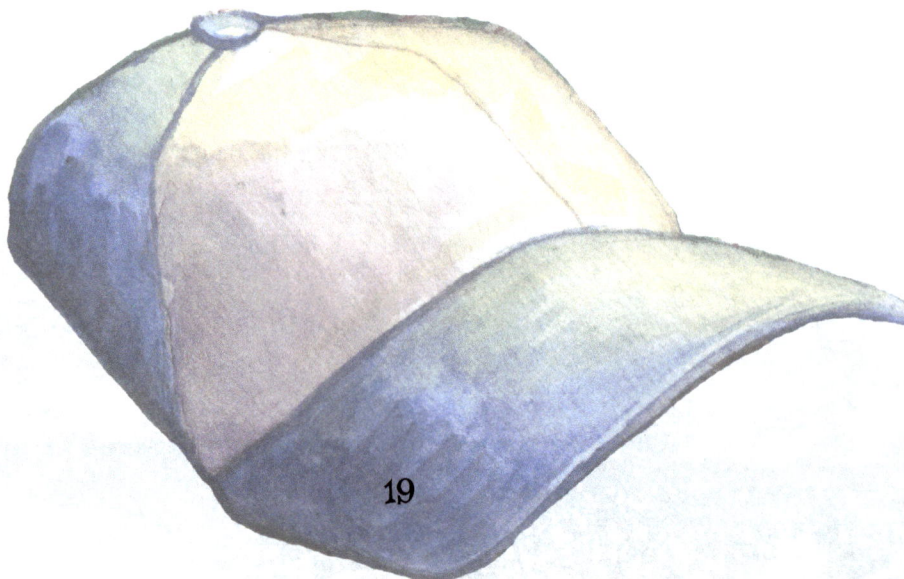

the doorbell to tell the neighboring little guy that our little guy couldn't play right then, stopped for a quick tinkle, then hopped in the car and made a dash to the fields, six miles away.

(Whew!)

We pulled up to the field ten minutes late and my little guy scrambled out of the car. He stood by the car door, new mitt in hand. Suddenly shy, he paused to survey the field full of kid sprouts, twelve in all, all no bigger than he. Then he walked by my side toward the infield – smiling and watching – full of hope and sap and heart.

I introduced him to the coach and he joined his teammates. I had planned to dash off and run errands, but what could I have been thinking? I turned and joined three moms in the dugout. They knew what I had almost forgotten. This was the first day of the rest of our little guys' lives, and we couldn't afford to miss it.

There was electricity pulsing in the air, a kind of spring madness. "My son was so cute when I told him I'd signed him up for baseball," one mom began. "He ran straight into the living room and slid right under the coffee table.

"When I asked him what he was doing, he said, 'I'm practicing! You have to slide a lot in baseball, and you have to practice.' He spent an hour and a half sliding under everything in the house – the dining table, his bed, the dog. I couldn't stop him . . . which was a bit hard on the dog."

"I can't wait till they try to hit the ball." I stood up to demonstrate how our middle son had looked when he'd started baseball. Some things never change, and the tee-baller's stance is one of them.

These ladies recognized it the moment I showed them – body bent over at the waist, bat swinging back and forth to improve the aim, eyes focused

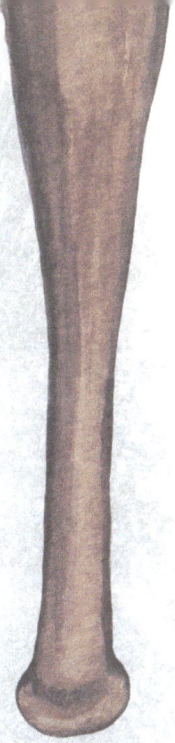

intensely on the ball, and tongue pointing straight out from the right side of the lips (for balance, maybe?).

Strike 22! And you're still not out! (No wonder they call the game on time, not innings.)

"Oh, look at him," a mom pointed at her kid. "He winds up three times before he throws it, every time. Isn't that funny?" We looked where she pointed, and sure enough, there stood a tow-headed dynamo, forearm rotating like a Popeye haymaker.

(One, two, three – whee!) Instinctively, we ducked.

"He could hit the target (in this case, the kid he played catch with), if he'd just nix the windup," she said. (We doubted it, but we let her keep her fantasy.) Actually, she was lying and we all knew it, but still we nodded. We knew the rules.

After several minutes of throwing and catching (well, throwing and fetching), Coach lined them all up at home plate to practice running the bases. A never-ending parade of little guys streamed around the bases, chasing one another like wind-up toys that never unwind. Soon, they all stacked up back at home plate 'till a whole wall of them toppled over, and the entire team fell like a line of dominoes.

"Good job, fellas!" called the coach. "Good hustle! You look great!"

Our kid sprout came home grinning, his freckle face peering out from under a large baseball cap that completely covered his ears. That night ole Freckle Face slept like a baby (well, he was a baby just a few days ago), while visions of caught balls danced in his head, and angelic grown-ups sang praises all night long.

Thus began our season in tee ball – our springtime journey into the little guys' very own field of dreams.

Visions of caught balls danced in his head, and angelic grown-ups sang praises all night long.

5
MMQ:
On Pest Control

In that long heat wave during that ghastly summer, we all sizzled like bacon on a griddle. Ouch! The grass stayed green in only the most well-watered places, and everything else turned brown and died.

Except for the ants.

The ants built freeways in the irrigation pipes, set up condos in the sprinkler heads, and established a merry-go-round in the water meter box (yippee!). These crafty critters survived major floods every other day, for 40 days and 40 nights, just as if they were God's chosen ants, a holy bug-nation.

We wondered if they might be Noahnese ants.

Each time the sprinkler clock in the garage would advance forward and we'd hear a valve clunk open, we'd hustle outside to see which sprinkler heads weren't working. We loved to watch the ants in a panic, streaming out of sprinkler heads in long refugee lines, carrying whatever stock and store they could, and running for their lives.

But once the floodwaters subsided, they moved right back in to the flood plains and built again. (Huh!?) That's when we began to think they might be idiot ants.

But soon, we decided they could, in fact, be Einsteinian ants.

After all, it takes some intelligence to sneak into a house through a closed kitchen window, and that's how our ants first arrived inside. Apparently, they'd decided to move to higher ground, in search of dry building

sites near water.

"Well, how about Mary Mary Quite's kitchen sink?"

"Say, that'll do nicely. Good thinking!"

I showered the window sill with enough ant spray to take down a burglar and thought I'd won when I hadn't seen any of their scouts for two days. But on the third day, I discovered twin ant highways running out of the wall plugs on either side of the kitchen window and leading directly back to my kitchen faucet.

Outside, right under the window, I found two miniature orange detour signs with arrows pointing down to the foundation, three feet below. They'd tunneled under the house and come up inside the wall!

They had planned it!

That's "E" for effort, "A" for planning, and "A+" for following directions. (Everything I ever needed to learn, I learned from the ants in my wall plugs.)

I turned on the tap and black ants rained like kamikaze pilots out of the pipe and onto the porcelain sink below. Yum! How about a nice tall drink of thrashing ants to quench your thirst on a hot summer's day?

Or perhaps you'd prefer to inhale the lovely odor of ant spray, when you've got the AC on, and all the windows are closed and it's 110° outside?

I kept spraying and held my breath 'till I saw my whole life flash before my eyes, but still the ants continued their assault on my kitchen – wave after wave – until finally, I just had to breathe. There were more of them than there were of me. (Duh.)

What I'd like to know is, once winter finally arrived and we had more rain than we needed, why were ants still invading my home, and this time in the shower of all places? Certainly, they didn't need water. And I sincerely doubt that they bathe.

But wait! I have a theory.

When F.W. Woolworth started his great chain of dime stores decades ago and was trying to drum up business, some underling in the shipping department convinced him to start carrying ant farms for sale.

(A forerunner of sea monkeys, no doubt.)

Adorable little kits they were, complete with two miniature plate glass windows that held an inch of sand between them.

A happy child would buy the kit, send away for a shipment of ants, and when they arrived, he would dump them inside, add sugar, then watch the tunnels take shape.

(Wow. And I get it all at home, for free!)

Well, I suspect that some of those domesticated ants escaped their farms (farms?) and bred with the wild ants, thereby creating a new Super Breed of ants, kind of the ant's version of killer bees. But these ants aren't killers, just squatters. Because

"Aaaah! There are ants in the shower! Look! Look!"

they think they should live inside our homes, not outside.

Get it?

They think they are pets, and every window or wall they encounter seems kinda homey to them and reminds them of the plate glass window/walls of their genetic ancestors, the Woolworthian ants.

As a matter of fact, I think they *like* being watched, and actually thrive on attention. See?

They liked it when we watched them whirl around on the water meter that summer. And they got a thrill out of all the fuss I made over them at my kitchen sink. If they had tails, they'd have been wagging them.

(Aha!)

And if ants really want to feel like members of the family, well, where's the one place where everyone will notice them sooner or later, and pay them lots of attention?

The shower stall.

"Aaaah! There are ants in the shower! Look! Look!"

So do not make the same mistake I made and encourage your ants. No. Because modern-day ants are neither Noahnese nor Einsteinian, but are in fact Woolworthian. And the way to rid your house of them is simply to ignore them.

Take. No. Notice.

Do not look at them. Ever!

Ignore the highways coming out of your window sills, your door jams, your pavement cracks, your wall plugs, your showers, your poor, your homeless. And, if your gaze does happen to light on some ants in, or near, your home, you must never, ever acknowledge their existence.

Don't say, "Wow!" or, "Oh my gosh!" or, "Look – ants!"

No, no, no!

Instead, practice walking around with your eyes closed, to show them how little you care.

And throw away your ant spray. Please!

Don't even think about calling an exterminator. (You might as well sign over the deed to your house.) Ants adore exterminators. It's like bringing an ambulance to a home for hypochondriacs.

"Ooh! Choose me, choose me!"

Ignore the ants in your home and pretend that they are not there, and they will simply pack up and leave. (Or die of neglect.) It's so easy! Of course, you may feel rather mean at first, making orphans out of them. But you'll get over it, and so will they.

Besides, your neighbors will probably give them all the attention they crave – and then some.

(A nuclear bomb, perhaps?)

6
MMQ:
On Great Meals
I Have Known

When old Hunk returns home from a business trip, we go through a full de-briefing of events. Were the flights on time? (Nope.) Were the meetings boring? (Yep.) Did someone, somewhere blow smoke in his face? (Always.) Did he miss me? (Abso-bloomin-lutely!) And did he miss my cooking?

Cooking? She cooks?

No.

She doesn't cook, and he didn't miss what she doesn't cook.

29

And then the real storytelling begins.

We've all watched this scene at least once in our lives, probably in an old Tarzan movie, or the like. Visualize the native hunter, wearing a loincloth and wielding a hand-hewn spear. He emerges from the jungle and stands before his tribe, arms raised in triumph. Behind him, fellow hunters trudge in a line, transporting a ferocious tiger, which once terrorized the village, but now is slain.

The dead beast swings from a long pole, to which all four feet are lashed. There are beating drums in the background, and a celebration is about to break out spontaneously, as an entire village gathers to pay homage to the great manly hunter.

This scene flashes through my mind's eye, each time Hunk comes home from a business trip and we surround him to celebrate his return from the urban jungle. He wields his trusty briefcase and carries in the proverbial bacon – contained not on a pole, but in a pay packet.

And then we, in turn, must gather to pay homage, and in the celebration that follows, also pay rapt attention to all the grisly details of the hunt.

Hunk's reenactment, in true tribal-hunter style, is acted out with the aid of dance, pulsating drums, sweeping gestures and animal skins, as the entire family gathers to hear yet another thrilling episode of that never-ending saga, "Great Meals I Have Known," by Hunk Huckstep.

You see, whenever he gets to dine on the company's credit card, Hunk seizes the opportunity to make up for all those lost calories back home, and gets down to some serious eating. Restaurants, then, are the main focus of Hunk's business forays and the primary compensation for having traveled out of town.

(And that's why he doesn't miss my cooking.)

When he returns back home again, this invariably leads to triumphant storytelling. And apparently, the experience isn't complete until it has been told.

Never having vowed to "love, honor, and cherish" their dad, the children abandon us early in the tale, leaving me to fend for myself against gastronomic descriptions that would leave even the most satiated being ravenous with hunger and wanting to stuff anything and everything within arm's reach into his mouth.

After thirty years in the business world, the all-time greatest meal Hunk ever knew came many years ago in New Orleans. All other meals before then, or after, are rated against this legendary meal.

(If New Orleans is a "10," then I'd rate St. Louis as a "7," etc.)

As legend would have it (and legend can take it!), this famed Mardi Gras meal was served in a private room, consumed in the company of prestigious computer moguls, and consisted of a mere twelve courses, all of which I've conveniently forgotten.

(No, wait! I remember – one of them was brown.)

It's not that I'm defensive about my cooking (or the lack thereof). No. Early in life it became apparent to me that I was only a two-trick pony and destined to remain so.

I can read and I can write. These are the talents with which I was born, and the talents with which I shall die.

But since I can also eat (a talent which is, alas, inevitable and unavoidable), I have endeavored to learn how to cook, simply as a matter of survival.

The results have never been too encouraging.

I was twelve when I first became aware that I was "domestically challenged." I had been spurred on by some moderate success in a junior

If the way to a man's heart was through his stomach, then I was in serious trouble.

high Foods class (well, my partner was Rachael Ray), and decided to try my luck at home and bake some cookies.

After reading the recipe, I was a little miffed to discover that it called for two cups of salt, and my mom had neglected to stock an adequate supply. I dutifully emptied out two salt shakers and the back-up container of salt into the measuring cup, and stirred the combined contents into the dough. Then I raided my piggy bank, hopped on my bike, and pedaled downtown to purchase more salt.

When I returned home and re-read the recipe to get my bearings, I realized that it had called for two cups of sugar, not salt. But that didn't faze me.

How could I counteract the effects of all that salt? Why, add extra sugar, of course. So I found a bag full of sugar, stirred that into the dough (whose consistency, by this time, curiously resembled Playdough), tasted it, decided it

needed even more sugar, then hopped on my bike to make yet another trip downtown.

By the time my cookie creations emerged from the oven, a noxious smell permeated the house and I had to open all the windows. Still, my mouth was watering in anticipation of my chewy confections. But once they cooled, I discovered that my cookies were as hard as stone and made my mouth pucker. I tried to convince my siblings to eat them, but the smell alone had turned them off.

In desperation, I gave them to the dog, who was legendary for eating stinky shoes, plastic toy soldiers, and poop. When he rejected my cooking, I knew it was hopeless. I was a walking culinary disaster and I always would be.

And if the way to a man's heart was through his stomach, then I was in serious trouble.

Fortunately, God is good and led me to a spouse whose

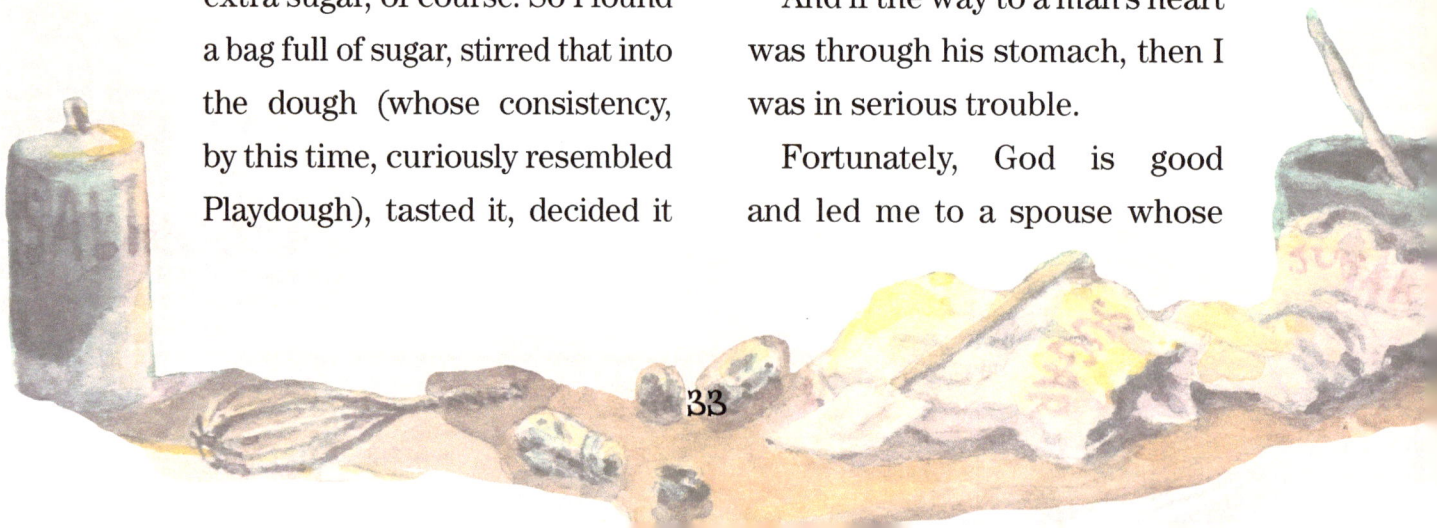

culinary talents are even worse than mine, who appreciates even the smallest effort on my part, and who is happy as long as I don't poison him.

(So far, so good!)

And the business trips help.

I'm just trying to figure out how I can travel with him. (After all, I'd like to have some good food once in a while, too. Ya know?)

Then perhaps I will write a revised version of this chapter. Perhaps I will call it "Great Meals We Have Known," or "They Also Get Served, Who in the Past Have Only Stood and Drooled."

NEW!

Babette

collect all six!

7
MMQ:
On Babette Dolls

*S*ometimes it helps to have a fresh perspective on life, and so I give you Hunk Huckstep and his sage remarks on Babette dolls. Take it away, Hunk!

There's a national movement afoot against the famous Babette doll! What? You didn't know? Well, of course you didn't. I just found out about it, myself.

The leaders of this underground terrorist movement are transported in my car to their elementary school, every weekday morning. They are four little boys who hate girls and detest anything even remotely associated with girls.

A note from MMQ: Now girls, don't take this personally. After all, these are little boys and they won't grow up until they're at least 33, so you just have to cut them some slack. Now, back to Hunk.

One morning, while making our daily trek to school at 7:15 a.m., I noticed that all four boys seemed to be asleep. I tried to engage them in conversation to get them to join the land of the living, so I asked them a couple of questions about the interesting things in their lives.

One boy volunteered that, "Some dumb girl brought her stupid Babette doll to school yesterday." Aha! They were showing signs of life.

So I seized the moment and asked them to dream up some new and improved Babette dolls, with descriptive names and unique characteristics. I made them adhere to one rule: Each doll's description must begin with the letter "B." Here is what their artful little brains invented –

Beanbag Babette is truly a versatile doll. She can be used for any sport requiring a ball. Why? Because she *is* the ball! When one boy drop-kicks her to another, she screeches like a cat, then clutches her forehead and moans for an hour. Boys also like to use her for a doorstop so they can constantly, accidentally, slam the door on her head.

Mildly alarmed, I asked the little sportsmen if they would ever attempt this with a real, live doll. "Oh no!" they chorused in horror. "Then we'd have to touch a girl, and girls have cooties!"

I must say, I was relieved to hear it.

Bubblebrain Babette just smiles and trills, "Ohmygosh!" in response to everything that is said to her. She loves all the music on the radio, but her absolute favorite is elevator muzak. Her main goal in life is to smile "that perfect smile" for twenty-eight hours straight, without relaxing her grin even once, in order to set the new World Smiling Record.

(The previous record was set in 1952 by Cheetah, Tarzan's pet chimpanzee.)

Bubblebrain comes complete with a battery-operated arm for extended waving sessions (which comes in handy during motorcades), a copy of *Pukey in Pink*, (which describes 1,000 things you can do with pink dye), and a package of post-it-notes, for her to write down her thought (in case she has one).

Belching Babette is a young boy's dream girl. She has no manners at all and happily embarrasses her entire family by belching on command. Her ensemble includes a stopwatch for timing her belches, a flip switch for choosing between Booming Burps or Bad-breath Belches, scorecards for rating belches 1 to 10, and an optional add-on unit to convert her into a Barfing Babette. And for just a few dollars more, you can obtain an Extra-Deep-Down Belch button.

(Wow, these boys were brilliant! Every enterprising tycoon knows where the money is – in accessories!)

Benchpress Babette can easily break your hand, just by shaking it. She can do anything a man can do, including shoving your head so far down into your shoulders that you'll be using your navel for an eye. So don't get on her bad side. She drives a ten-ton truck and likes to brag that it's the only tractor-trailer in the world without power steering.

(With a bicep bigger than Shaq's thigh, who needs power steering?)

Backstop Babette is used by boys when playing baseball and nobody wants to be catcher. Her face is slightly dished and grows more concave with each pitch. She also has a bright red target on her face, with the bull's eye between her eyes – not to be confused with Barfing Babette's zit button.

Warning: Timid readers who don't share the mind of a 10 year old boy might want to

This is the list the young hoodlums concocted,
and all in the ten-minute drive to school.

avert their eyes for the next two paragraphs. (Really!) MMQ

Barfing Babette pukes a slimy green substances when you push a red button in the middle of her forehead (lovingly called the zit button). The boys call the junk she barfs up "chunky green." She comes complete with a list of foods that make her sick, an Up-Chuck Bucket for heaving at home, and a Barf Bag for barfing while traveling.

There's also a doctor's little black bag, in case Barfing needs emergency treatment. It contains a tourniquet for her stomach, a syringe with a twelve-inch needle, and a ping pong paddle to use as a tongue depressor.

Knowing that each one of these boys had a mommy at home and a grandma nearby, I just had to interject: "You would never actually harm a real girl, right? Like Mom or Grandma?"

"Ewwww. Mom and Grandma aren't girls! That's just gross."

"Oh, okay. I just wanted to make sure . . . ."

So, this is the list the young hoodlums concocted, and all in the ten-minute drive to school. (It's amazing how quickly their little brains can work, when they want to.)

Meanwhile, stay tuned. I'm considering asking the boys to come up with a complementary set of dolls based on Babette's boyfriend, the Ben doll . . . .

And now, for a final thought from MMQ –

Folks, if this episode upset you, I have two words for you: Girl Juice!

Buy some today at your local elementary school, and spray it on all the sexist, disgusting, immature humor in this episode. In a mere ten seconds, all those disturbing images will morph into hearts, roses, butterflies, and baby's breath, and you will be transported back to the real Babette world.

(Please note that I did not say "the real world.")

8
MMQ:
On Easter Eggs

I didn't waste time trying to understand. After all, a girl has to catch on quickly, if she wants to get ahead. The authority figures in lavender dresses and gray suits had simply changed their minds, that's all. And there had been no warning. But hey, I didn't care.

I was ecstatic.

"You want me to eat candy?" I can do that.

"You want to show me where the candy's hidden?" Wow, somebody pinch me.

"You want me to find as much candy as I can, as fast as I can?"

Yippee! The grown-ups have been replaced by aliens!

Let's race around like maniacs

and swallow as much sugar as we can, before the grown-ups come back and claim their bodies!

It was a child's preview of heaven, Saint Barnabus Episcopal Church on that Easter Sunday morning, those many moons ago. Of course, the good Reverend Whatchamacallit had gone on a bit about sin and blood and other grown-up stuff that morning. But afterwards, he took me by the hand and led me to a miniature chocolate egg, wrapped up in green foil, which had been placed in a low branch of the oak tree outside the church.

"Look! Here's one for you," he smiled. "See how many more you can find."

And they're off!

It was open season on Easter eggs, as a hoard of screaming children hoisted their baskets and started running neck-and-neck and living hand-to-mouth.

I spotted a pink egg lying on top of a flat rock, but Jimmy Spoiler appeared out of nowhere and grabbed it before I could even stretch out my hand.

Not fair! Jimmy Spoiler was a bully!

Then I saw Toddling Teddy wobble over toward a sprinkler head. Hmmm. If I hustled a bit and slid . . . . Crash!

Ha hah! Victory was mine. The egg was mine!

Tough toenails, Teddy! If you snooze, you lose. (Told you I was a quick learner.)

This touching Easter scene took place several decades ago, when I was only five. But some things never change.

(Human greed, for one.)

Some folks say that to be a good parent, a person must have a good memory. So that's why, when old Hunk and I were raising kids and finally had a yard big enough for egg hunts, we designated a side yard by the grapevines as the special place for pre-schoolers to hunt their eggs.

But that was our second year.

The first year was an entirely different story – in more ways than one!

The Saturday before our first annual Easter egg hunt, I met a young mom and her two kids in front of our house. We introduced ourselves and chatted, then I invited her to join us at 3:00 pm the next day for our egg hunt. It would give us a chance to meet her parents, our neighbors across the street. Our passel of rascals were already pumped for the big day – along with a few of the neighboring kids – and a couple more egg hunters would be welcome.

But when I answered the doorbell at 3:00 pm on Easter Sunday, 25 strange people filed into my house, grinning and nodding. The kids carried empty baskets and the grown-ups carried cameras.

"Who are all these people?" old Hunk whispered in my ear.

"Beats me!" I whispered back. But they looked friendly, so I smiled at them. "How nice to see you . . . all of you. Who are you!?"

"We're here for the egg hunt," said a man with glasses. "This is Sally and Priscilla (she's due in June) and Hank and baby Sue and Billy and . . . ."

Oh my gosh, where did they all come from?

A familiar face appeared in the crowd, the mom from the previous day.

"Hello, Mary. This is our family! We get together every Easter. Thanks for inviting us." Then the doorbell rang again, and I jumped.

Heaven help us.

But it was only the three boys from next door, and they were expected. The oldest boy held out a sack full of plastic eggs. "You can hide these, too," he offered. Aha! Here was an answer to prayer before I even

had a chance to pray.

I thanked him, glommed onto his bag, and wove my way through my crowded living room. (Excuse me. Oh, sorry. Sooo sorry!) Then I dumped the contents of all four of my candy dishes into that bag.

Next, I grabbed my own garbage sack full of eggs and pulled all the blinds closed. Then I steered old Hunk (who looked rather glassy-eyed at this point) and our oldest son outside, where I asked them to hide over three hundred eggs. And do it quick, before someone suffocated in our tiny living room.

Fifteen minutes later, our half-acre was in chaos.

A three-year-old girl in a party dress sat in the mud, eating chocolate and tin foil.

"Smile for the camera!" Mommy focused and clicked.

A two-year-old boy wandered right past three eggs at eye level, inches from his face.

"Look!" Daddy pointed at the eggs, then his video camera whirred.

School-aged kids tramped through my sweet peas and emerged grinning, arms full of colored eggs and torn blossoms.

Then Jimmy Spoiler appeared and stole an egg from our youngest boy. And the tears flowed like Niagara Falls.

Old Hunk planted his hand over the egg and gave Jimmy *The Dad Look*. Ooooh!

"Say you're sorry."

"Sorry."

"Now give him back his egg."

The egg was dutifully returned.

Then pandemonium reigned once again!

We loved it. (We found stray eggs right up until Labor Day.)

The next year, we had the same group over again, and it felt like old home week. This time, everybody brought eggs.

And we posted nightclub bouncers at either end of the pre-schoolers' plot, to keep out the Jimmy Spoiler in us all.

(Well, it worked!)

We posted nightclub bouncers at either end
of the pre-schoolers' plot, to keep out the Jimmy Spoiler in us all.

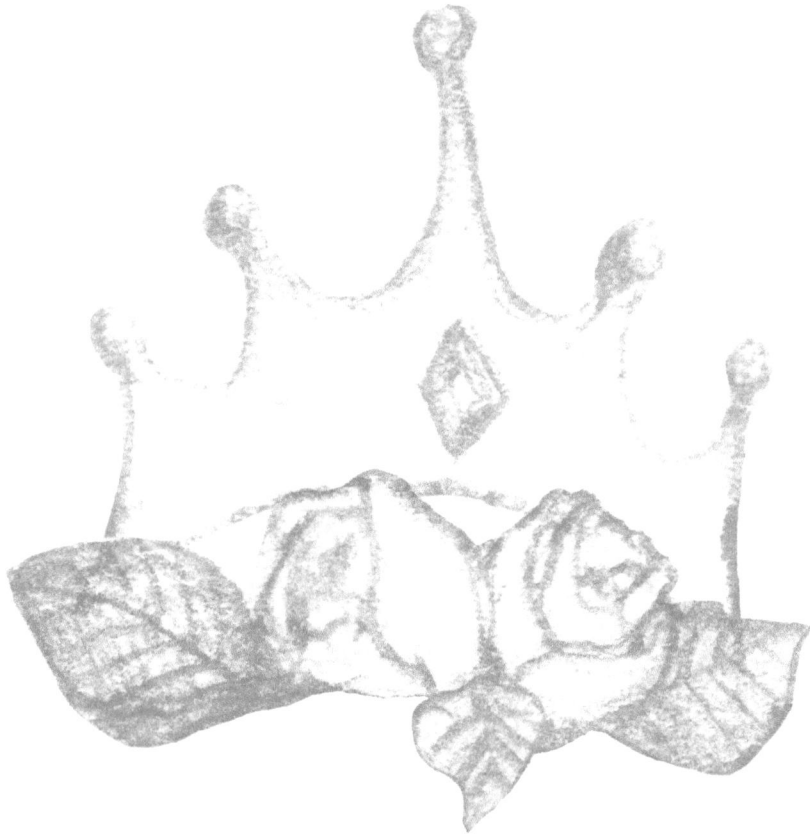

9
MMQ:
On Females and Prom

Henry David Thoreau once wrote, "Beware of enterprises which require a suit of new clothes." Fortunately, he never said a word about dresses.

Girls spend months planning for prom, and finding the perfect dress early in the process is absolutely crucial. If a girl has not bought her prom dress by the end of Spring Break (or May 1st at the very latest), then a special type of insanity is sure to set in, known in the medical profession as *Absensio-Dresso-*

Phobia, or ADP, for short.

The early warning signs of ADP are unmistakable, for when the afflicted female travels within two miles of a mall, she cannot control the urge to hang her head out the car window and pant like a dog. Anyone who observes these symptoms in a friend or loved one must administer emergency treatment immediately, or the ADP sufferer cannot be held responsible for her actions.

Do not pass Go.

Do not collect $200.

Floor it!

Speed like the dickens to the nearest dress store and make that girl shop. For if you don't, then she will begin to bark and growl and tear flesh like a werewolf. This beastly behavior will not cease until the poor tortured soul has trotted into a fancy dress shop, pawed at least a dozen prom dresses, looked into six mirrors, and whimpered to two girlfriends on her cell phone.

ADP victims possess an uncanny ability to sniff out prom dresses at the front door of a store, where they will point, strike a pose, then freeze into place to indicate to all concerned that the prey has been spotted, and that they should hoist their credit cards and charge.

But the victim should not be allowed to rush right in. No!

For if given too much of a lead, the young lady might actually sprout a tail and begin to wag it. This is an extremely serious development, and the only known cure is to spend hundreds of dollars as quickly as possible.

The worse case of ADP ever documented was in Seattle, in 1996, when a young lady was found on all fours, scratching fleas and baying at the moon outside of her local Nordstrom department store at 3:00 in the morning, the day of her senior prom.

Her story is tragic.

She had broken up with her boyfriend a month before prom and had given her dress to a friend, but when she and her boyfriend made up two weeks later, she found herself back in the count-down, weeks behind schedule, and bereft of a dress.

The poor thing was doomed.

When the police carted her off, she was baring her teeth and growling, "I do believe in fairy godmothers. I do believe in fairy godmothers. I do, I do, I do, I doooo!"

My fellow Americans! Is this fair?

Should females have all the stress?

Why must gals suffer for the sake of a big occasion, and never guys? After all, this is the new millennium! There should be equal strokes for both gals and guys – yes?

Guys go to only one shop and simply rent their tuxes. It takes 15 minutes, max. And if three or four guy-friends all go together and rent exactly the same tuxedos, what do we do? We applaud their male-bonding.

(Oh, aren't they precious.)

But why?

Because every female knows that if she sees someone else wearing the same prom dress she's wearing, the one that took her three months and sixteen shopping malls to find, then her entire evening is ruined. Ruined, I tell you!

Is this fair?

Why can't girls rent their dresses? A girl could wear a different prom dress to school each day for a week, hand out coupons to all her girlfriends, and earn a free rental dress for herself.

(But she could still surprise her date. He could have tons of fun guessing: Which day of the week will she wear on our big night out?)

Or – imagine a girl's mother nagging away, reminding her that prom is only a week away and she'd better go rent her dress

Our Prom

The worst case of ADP ever documented was in Seattle, in 1996.

before all the killer deals are gone, and she has to pay more than $50 for her entire outfit.

(Hah! That'll be the day!)

It's sooo not fair.

In addition to dresses, girls have to find fingernails, fingernail polish, fancy undergarments, slinky nylons, dazzling earrings, dainty dancing shoes, a darling evening bag, a delectable evening wrap, a dynamite make-up job, a flawless hairdo and a flirty hair decoration. Imagine finding the perfect dress, and all that extra junk in only one rental store, and in only fifteen minutes.

(Yeah, right. Bibbity bobbity boo!)

Let's face it. Women have been stressing over their looks since the dawn of time, back when Eve grabbed that first fig leaf, and Adam uttered those now-famous words, words which have reverberated throughout the corridors of time –

"Honey, you look real good in green."

From that moment on, we were hooked.

A few centuries later came the Cinderella incident and the first recorded case of ADP behavior in a female. Scholars tell us that the earliest Dead-Cee scrolls all indicate that Cindy was out in the garden *baying*, when her fairy godmother arrived to save her from certain insanity. But due to a transcription error, the word "crying" was substituted for "baying" and the real Cinderella story was lost forever.

The rest is fairytale history.

(But now that I think of it, Cindy's story also shows the importance of having the perfect pair of shoes . . . which is yet another story.)

Be kind to the females in your midst during prom season, folks. If a girl can survive prom unscathed, then there is hope for her future. She just might make it through her marriage ceremony without trotting down the aisle on all-fours.

10
MMQ:
On Getting Organized

*O*nce more, I hand the MMQ reins over to that wise, homespun philosopher, Hunk Huckstep. Now, let's see what's on his mind . . . .

One day, Mary and I grew weary of seeing the walls closing in on our younger sons' rooms. Those two boys were the kings of clutter.

In several overflowing laundry baskets, dirty clothes blended indistinguishably with clean. Half-finished projects peeked out from under their beds, in an odd assortment of good intentions gone wrong.

Cub Scout memos, Monopoly cards, dirty dishes, math

homework, tissue clumps, dog biscuits, magic tricks, mosquito repellent, CD covers, and a mish-mash of generic junque covered every horizontal surface in their rooms, and even some of the vertical surfaces.

We couldn't tell anymore whether or not the rooms were even carpeted.

Each boy's room cried out, "Help me, help me! I'm suffocating!"

Finally, we decided to take pity on those poor, neglected domiciles.

And so began a process that enlightened me on some of the basic differences between Mary and me. It also provided a valuable lesson that would help me keep my sanity and my marriage intact for decades to come.

Mary's reaction to the boys' rooms was to ask me to run out and buy two dozen cigar boxes. These would hold all the smaller items that boys tend to collect –

used toothpicks; water-logged baseball cards; pencil stubs; gum wrappers that might someday prove useful; mangled, wallet-sized photos of unidentifiable friends; minute pieces of wire; fossilized orange rinds and apple cores; model airplane pieces; used Band-Aids; fingernail clippings; and of course, parts of animals.

Each box would hold things and be labeled, to make it easier for the boys to ignore.

I knew a lost cause when I saw one. You don't organize a boy's room – you purge it with fire! I mean, you gotta throw away 100 pounds of crud for every 50 pounds you keep, or you make no progress. And I said so to Mary.

I stated that, as head of the house, I would direct the tidying of the rooms my way, and that was that. Then I got in my car, went to the drug store, and purchased two dozen cigar boxes.

You don't organize a boy's room –
you purge it with fire!

Labeling the boxes wasn't sufficient for Mary. She also made Velcro fastenings for each box, to keep it securely closed. This consumed the better part of two days, got Mary off schedule on all her other projects, and put her into a state of permanent time warp.

She stayed two days behind herself for the next three years, until she finally got the idea to add two extra sheets of days to her flip calendar and morphed herself out of her warp. (Really.)

True to form (and my predictions), the boys never did use the cigar boxes. But the boxes did add a certain air of organization to their closets. It was kind of like having your shoes in a perfect dress-right-dress line, while the rest of the room looked like World War Three had hit.

After the dust had settled (literally), it finally occurred to me that Mary and I had stumbled upon something important and had discovered one of the fundamental differences between us.

When Mary organizes, she looks for more containers to hold the junk overflowing from bureaus, bookcases, and closets. When I organize, I throw away as much junk as possible in order just to see the bureaus, bookcases, and closets. Then, and only then, do I try to bring order to what is left. Sometimes, in my enthusiasm, I even throw out the bureaus, bookcases, and closets.

All this has caused me to see

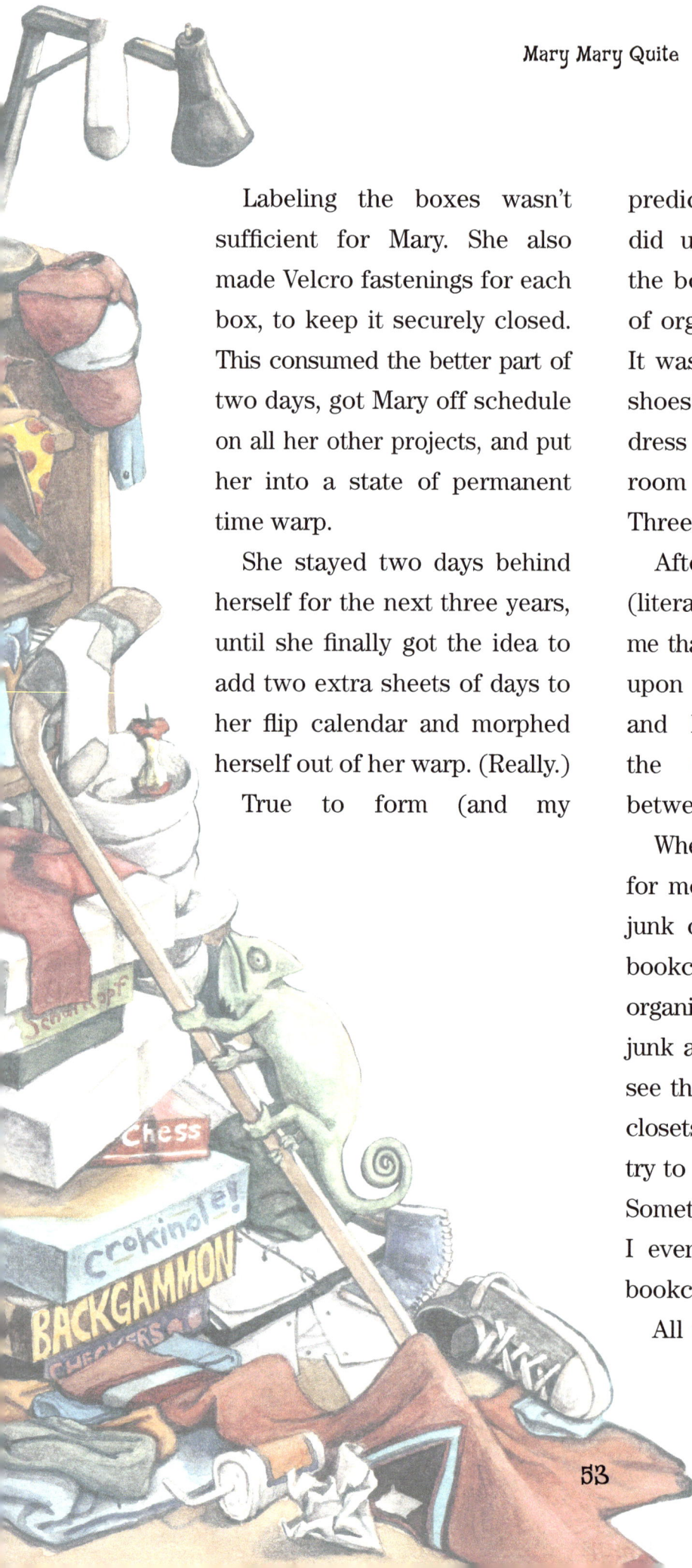

Mary in a different light.

I now know what when she says, "Let's clean the garage," she really means, "Let's see if we have room in your closet for the ping pong table, thirteen artificial Christmas trees, a pile of discarded pots and pans, various bicycle parts, four tons of camping equipment, and other sundry garbage. But first, let's buy lots of big boxes to hold all this trash."

My new reaction to any organizational overtures from Mary is to try to postpone anything at all, until the idea has faded from her memory.

Using my standard ploy, I instantly reply, "Is that a hijacked plane overhead? Are we at war? New dress? It's really lovely. What's your main goal in life? Would you take the job as head of IBM if they offered it to you? How long is string? Do you think Freud had nightmares, or just dreams? Want to go out to dinner tonight at an extremely expensive restaurant?"

By the time I end my jabbering, she has heard only my last question, says "Yes," and forgets anything having to do with getting organized.

Thus, I have saved our marriage by avoiding having to reconcile all the differences in our approaches to getting organized. For that would be much more difficult than actually cleaning the boys' rooms.

Note from MMQ: Hah! If those cigar boxes were so useless, then why did one of them make it into your briefcase as a permanent fixture, huh Hunk?

(And yes, I do love to have the last word. Besides, it's my book!)

11
MMQ:
On The
MOB App

It's the most annoying thing on the planet and I'm really upset about it. When I die and go to heaven, I'm gonna ask God what on earth He was thinking. And I don't mind telling you, He's gonna get an earful.

So what's my beef?

Why, oh why, can't mamas live their kids' lives for them? Huh?

Think about it. It would solve so many problems before they even started. And it would save so many kids from making mistakes. Big, hairy, dumb-dumb mistakes. And it would certainly give all us hard-working mamas a break.

Lord knows, we need a break.

I'm not talking about a break that takes you to the ER, either. Nope. We need a break from the trauma of seeing our kids mess up.

Dear God, life would be so simple, if only we had a Mama On Board, magical, instantaneous, high-powered, panic App. (Otherwise known as the MOB App.)

Yes! That would do the trick and nicely.

Think about it.

Your little sweetheart is out on the soccer field, hustling down the sideline, and closing in on the goal. The ball comes straight at him. He kicks, he misses – the ball that is – and the other team squirrels it far, far away from your poor little wannabe.

But if you could just leap out there and kick the ball for your baby – and of course, you would never miss – then dash back before anyone saw you, why then your child could have the thrill, the joy, the ecstasy of actually connecting with the ball. He or she would gain confidence, feel good about himself, and maybe even score a goal next time.

Woo hoo!

What would be the harm in that?

Hey presto, Mama On Board!

No.

Absolutely, positively, not.

You need to forget about the mamas on the other teams.

No, I really don't care about those other mamas.

Their athletic offspring can stand on their own two feet, and they don't need any intervention, at all. Thank you very much.

The MOB App is only for the kids who can't kick the ball, quite yet. You know, it's for the slow starters, the late bloomers, the – now you've forced me to say it – the losers.

Hey, but with the MOB App, no child would be a loser for long.

Ta-da!

And if your kid's already a good athlete, just think about the other things you could do with my soon-to-be-famous Mama On Board, magical, instantaneous, high-powered, panic App – or its advanced version, the Father on Board, magical, instantaneous, high-powered panic App, also known as the FOB App.

What if Dad told your little darlin' that she can't go to the birthday party unless she cleans her room? Then when it's time to leave – her bed's a mess, muddy clothes cover the floor, her trashcan's a toxic waste dump, and her hamster's lying there, goggle-eyed and belly-up, on a pile of urine-soaked wood chips?

And Dad? Why, he just spent twenty bucks on an over-priced set of Cinderella slippers, and all he really wants to do is knock back a coupla beers with the Birthday Girl's dad, while their daughters go whacko at the party, getting high on sugar.

So, what's a Dad to do? Why, bring out the FOB App, of course.

Only this time, it's not Dad who cleans up your child's room in a nano-second. Oh, no. This time, your child does all the work. Every last lick of it. And with all the obsessive-compulsive excellence of Mr. Clean on speed. Ta-da!

Hey presto, Father On Board!

Now, just in case you're thinking that the MOB/FOB App would be effective only for interfering in the lives of little children, let me explain just how helpful it will be when raising teenagers.

"But Mom," your brilliant teenager complains, "I don't want to go to college. I already know everything there is to know, and if I discover something that I don't know, then I'll just Google it. I will not fill out those college applications and you can't make me."

Good Lord, what's a mama to do?

The kid's too old for the Naughty Chair, too young to throw out on his ear, and if you send him to his room, he'll just plug into his iPod and disappear into la-la land. But wait! Help is on the way.

Hey, presto! It's Mama On Board!

Only this time, when you use the MOB App, the most amazing thing happens. And let me tell you, it's worth waiting all those years, just to see it.

Cuz this time, you get to

This time your child does all the work. Every last lick of it.

change your child's brain. His thinking. His skull! Isn't that wonderful? And it's what you've really wanted all along – secretly – now isn't it.

Yep, I thought you'd fess up, once you knew the power that the MOB App had in store for you.

You simply whip out your handy, Mama On Board, magical, instantaneous, high-powered panic App, aim it at your confused teenager, press it – and ta-da! Suddenly, you've put an old head on young shoulders. Isn't that fabulous? It's everything you've ever dreamed of doing, but forgot to ask for.

Suddenly, your teen is saying things like, "Did you remember to pay the house insurance?" and, "It looks like it might rain, I'd better take an umbrella." Oh, and this one's my personal favorite: "Gee, you look tired. Why don't you go take a nap, and I'll put the groceries away."

Hey, presto! Mama's On Board

and the kid's got a brain!

(Just a quick note of caution, here: Please use sparingly, or your teen could morph into a Stepford child.)

So, now that I've pleaded my case with all you moms and dads out there, I'm sure you'll all agree with me that the MOB/ FOB App is something that a brilliant scientist, somewhere on this planet, needs to invent and right away. Of course, if his or her mama really did have a MOB App, then just think how easy it would be to get that first one made.

(Well, that made perfect sense to *me*.)

Hey, look!

Mama's little brainiac just invented the very first Mama On Board, magical, instantaneous, high-powered, panic App!

Hmmmmm. There's only one hitch, as far as I can see.

And that's figuring out just how that mama's gonna find a way to make her awesome little genius do what she wants him or her to do – like invent the MOB App – in the first place.

(Because, if left to their own devices, those little geniuses might just invent the KOB App – Kid on Board – and control their parents, instead.)

Yowser!

So, is there anybody else out there with any other brilliant ideas?

12
MMQ:
On Mother's Day

others . . . you can't live with 'em and you can't live without 'em. (Think about it.)

Mothers . . . you just gotta love 'em.

Siblings, however, know that it's always open season on mothers. This is because moms, by job description, are authority figures. And every youngster, by job description, is a rebel.

So that is why, when my brother was ten and studying history, he took my sister and me down to a remote corner of the garden where he knew it would be safe, then shared his subversive insight: "Mommy is Hitler," he whispered.

We all snickered and he started barking orders in a little-boy falsetto.

I glanced over my shoulder,

then goose-stepped toward him, whispering, "Heil Mommy!"

Mom. Will we ever recover from her maternal war crimes?

Hitler commanded her soldiers to change their underwear and eat their broccoli, and we – in blind obedience – did what we were told!

But it wasn't our fault, honest! We were just following orders!

(Well . . . sometimes we followed orders.)

Three years after my brother's alarming insights, when I was fifteen and my mother forty, Mommy arranged a water-skiing trip for the entire family. We loaded up the station wagon, drove to The Lake, set up camp, then talked to the locals about learning how to ski. The next day we rented a boat, drove out to the middle of the lake, and in I jumped.

The ski belt kept me afloat while I slipped on the skis, then Dad steered the boat so the rope floated right beside me and I grabbed it. Next, I positioned my ski-tips so they stuck up out of the water in front of me, placed the rope's handlebar between the skis, hung on with both hands, and yelled, "Hit it!"

The boat lurched forward and so did I. But I couldn't get my butt up and out of the water on that first attempt. My face met a wall of water and I had to let go or drown. (I let go.)

"Try keeping your seater up," Mommy coached.

(Now, why didn't I think of that?)

It took me three tries, but soon I was up and skiing. My brother learned by watching me, and he was skiing in only two tries, as was my sister.

Next, came Mommy's turn.

She put on the ski belt, jumped in the lake, and we handed her the skis.

Remember those old black and white movies where Johnny Weissmuller plays Tarzan? There's one scene that's in at least three of those movies, where Tarzan wrestles a man-eating crocodile, while both man and beast whirl 'round and 'round in a river, thrashing in mortal combat. One moment Tarzan's on top of the water; the next he's underneath, wildly stabbing at the croc until (of course) he conquers the beast.

It was this particular scene that flashed through my mind as I watched Mommy trying to put on her skis. She thrashed and whirled and stabbed for a good twenty minutes before – finally – she conquered those twin crocs.

(Ooom-gowah, Mommy!)

Meanwhile, we three kids enjoyed The Mommy Show – pointing, falling against each other, and cackling like witches.

Double, double, Mommy's in trouble. He-he! He-he! Heeeee!

(My, what sweet children.)

Finally, Mommy got herself in position and yelled, "Hit it!" and actually stood up on her very first try. (Way to go, Mommy!) Only she didn't stay up. She went up, back, and all the way over, her entire body rotating backwards in slow motion – skis and all.

We three witches stared in amazement, spellbound. Then we underwent a magical transformation. We stuck out our necks, threw our snouts wide open, and brayed like mules.

Hee-haaaw! Hee-haaaw!

Ten more times Mommy yelled, "Hit it!" and ten more times she stood up, fell back, and went tail-end over teakettle.

Each time Mommy fell backwards, failing, we three mules fell forwards, braying. She continued to try and fail, while we continued to hee-haw and grow more beastly.

We thought she was hilarious.

We never asked her what she thought.

It took me three tries to learn to ski. It took Mommy three days. But she did it. I was fifteen and fit. She was forty and a fighter.

And now that I'm also over

Ten more times Mommy yelled, "Hit it!" and ten more times she stood up,
fell back, and went tail-end over teakettle.

forty (just a bit, mind you), I'm ashamed of my asinine behavior. But I do have more empathy now than I did back then – when I never, ever thought that I, too, would someday . . . actually . . . be . . . (gulp) . . . forty.

Sorry, Mom.

(But watching The Mommy Show was really good for sibling bonding!!)

And I'm proud of my mother. Because that same fighting spirit that pushed her past failure and got her up and skiing – made her push me past failure, and got me up and . . . well, up and out the door!

When I was in elementary school, she wouldn't let me pick my nose, no matter how much I loved the taste of boogers. And there was no way she'd let me quit piano lessons, no matter how much I stamped my foot and hollered.

When I was in high school, did she ask me if I did my homework? No. She asked my teachers. (The nerve of that woman!) Going to college was non-negotiable, and she even insisted that I pay back the two bucks she loaned me to buy a sparkly pen when I was twelve.

(Dear God, the abuse.)

Heil Mommy!

You went about the business of mothering the same way you went about everything else in life. You fought for what was right for the people you loved – even if you had to fight the people you loved, to make them do what was right!

(You know what, Mommy? *You da man!*)

A person could do a lot worse than have a dictator for a mom. (Unless, of course, you are forty and she still picks out your clothes.)

13

MMQ:
On Teenage Driving

Teenage driving. It's all about freedom and independence.

And then again, it's also about slavery and increased dependence, too – passing that test and getting that first driver's license.

Each one of our kids has been, understandably, ecstatic.

"I passed! I got my license!" each one would yell, holding the magical temporary license up in the air with one hand, while doing high-fives all 'round with the other. Then followed the obligatory family celebration and the traditional spin over to a friend's house for the first solo flight.

Heaven.

It felt like heaven . . . until reality set in.

Sometimes reality would come in the form of red and blue lights flashing in the rearview mirror.

Other times it came in the form of working after-school jobs to pay for insurance.

But the most dreaded reality check of all has been the accidents, also known as, "Whoops! Crunch and Munch. How did that happen?"

In this category the boys seem to have fared worse than the girls, although I understand from talking to other parents that Crunch and Munch is not necessarily gender-specific, by nature.

But think about it. We encourage aggression in our male offspring, so why are we surprised when it surfaces behind the wheel?

How many of us holler, "Hit him hard!" when our sons are playing football? Or hoot in triumph when they pin their wrestling opponents to the mat? ("Way to go, Slammer!")

So why are we so shocked when our boys treat driving a car like it's just another contact sport? If it is, then Crunch and Munch actually makes perfect sense.

Collision avoidance detectors?! No way!

They wanna score some points.

SHAKA-BAM!!! "Gnarly crash, dude!"

(You know what I mean.)

And how about telling the little rascals to speed like the dickens at a track meet, or to run like blazes around the bases? Hey, seems like our little adrenaline junkies have caught on pretty good, now doesn't it?

So, why are we parents complaining?

(I know, we've earned the right to complain, cuz we pay the bills.)

Seems like our little adrenaline junkies have caught on pretty good, now doesn't it?

(So . . . does that mean our kids get to complain, once they start paying for those inevitable Crunch and Munch bills?)

Okay, okay! I was only kidding!

Our oldest son took our brand new Toyota free-wheeling on a dirt fire-truck road in the hills outside our home, and ran straight into a – you guessed it – fire truck.

Whoops! Crunch and Munch. How did that happen?

Our middle son took the same car, or I should say, the same car's replacement (affectionately named "Yoda"), and rolled it down a three-hundred foot driveway. He and his girlfriend had been sitting and talking in the car one minute (at least he claims that they were talking), then after he had walked her to her door and come back again, Yoda had simply disappeared.

Whoops! Crunch and Munch. How did that happen?

Maybe he should have set the parking brake. Or maybe he should have listened to his dad's advice, whose mantra has always been, "Leave the car in gear, never in neutral. It's safer that way."

"Well gee, Dad. The gear shift knob and the parking brake get in the way sometimes."

"Mmm hmmm. I want you to pay me for the damages. I need the cash."

And speaking of cash . . . now that I think of it, there is one thing about our girls that has been a little Whoopsy, even if they haven't had an official Crunch and Munch. Cuz the girls can never seem to find the cash to pay for gas – thereby giving Mom or Dad a fun surprise.

"Gee Mom, I thought I had three quarters in the bottom of my purse, but I couldn't find them, so I came straight home instead of putting gas in the car."

"Yes dear, and what century are you living in? I want you to borrow Dad's car, drive to the gas station, buy five whole dollars worth of gas, and bring it to me at the bottom of Rollercoaster Hill. And hurry. I have to go to the bathroom."

Since our youngest son inherited a bruised, battered, and rusting vehicle, perhaps that's why he has never had a Crunch and Munch to his name. And he's been driving for some time, now. Perhaps he's learned from his older siblings' mistakes. Or perhaps he's just plain fortunate.

But to tell you the truth, we're getting to be a bundle of nerves around here.

You see, we're used to hearing from Mr. Calamity Crunch, since he's come visiting with such regularity. And when he hasn't shown his face for a while, we get a bit nervous.

It's kind of like being a kid and getting in trouble and knowing you deserve to be disciplined. "Come on," you feel like saying, "just give me my punishment and get it over with. I know I deserve it, so just do it."

Whoops! Did I say that? (How did that happen?) Please, Mr. Crunch, Sir, I was only kidding!

14
MMQ:
On Moving Out

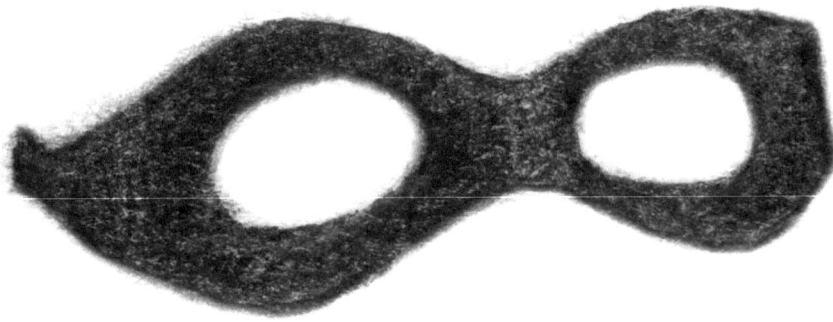

Each time one of our children leaves home, my husband and I experience a great sense of loss.

When our oldest son got married and moved out, we lost two laundry baskets, a rechargeable flashlight, and three thermal blankets. Our maple dresser went on permanent loan, and the Visa card on temporary.

No problem – we got to keep our son's dog.

Not to be outdone, his older sister reached for greater, unscaled heights. When she left home, she took our car.

The latest one to make her move has been our younger daughter, the Newlywed. Into her love nest, she's taken our portable TV (recently returned in favor of her brother's castoff console), six pairs of my sport socks, and our card table with folding chairs. Knowing that I am rather fond of my card table, she lets me come over and visit it, sometimes.

It looks lonely in her apartment.

I find myself haunting garage sales and thrift shops, searching for a cheap dining set for darling Newly. When I find one, I'll buy it for her. And then – oh the joy of being reunited with my card table!

After all, it's practically a member of the family.

Sometimes, I just miss my stuff, ya know?

But really, how could we have known – all those years ago when we brought our darling little babies into the world – that they were all, in fact, kleptomaniacs?

Cute, cuddly, incurable little kleptos.

Born with sticky fingers.

What's yours is mine and what's mine is mine.

And why can't they steal the junk we don't want? Like that barking puppy-dog clock we got from Aunt Whosits? Or the rug

that slides across the floor each time I step out of the shower? And what about our lifetime collection of empty mayo jars? I'd manage just fine without all that junk – the things that nobody else wants, either. (Wah.)

But hey, it's not that I mean to complain. (Not much, anyway.)

It's just a little confusing, that's all.

You see, our children are actually honest people. And when they said, "We're independent and ready to face the world on our own," my husband and I were easily led.

We believed them.

But sometimes I wonder if it hasn't all been a discreet act of kindness on their parts. Could they have actually felt obligated to borrow from us?

The taking of a few sticks of furniture, or a temporary set of wheels, could have been their way of being easy on us, of slowly weaning us from our need to be providers. Perhaps

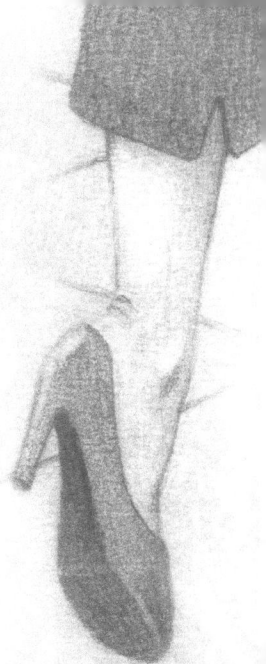

Cute, cuddly, incurable little kleptos. Born with sticky fingers.

they realized that it might take time for us to adjust to not being needed anymore.

Well, how considerate of them!

Just in case my theory might be true, old Hunk and I decided to call their bluff. We told them that we had made the adjustment. We no longer needed to be needed, and they could give us back our stuff.

Strange.

Just last week, we had a nice tidy garage. Suddenly, it's jam packed with all kinds of rubbish we've never seen before.

Someone has barricaded the path to my freezer with a huge yellow motorcycle. It sits there on two flat tires, like a big, banana-colored slug.

Did we loan somebody a motorcycle?

I don't recall that we ever had a motorcycle to loan. And I'm pretty sure we never owned a 30's style dining table and sideboard, four orange leather chairs, and a boa constrictor in a terrarium.

Did we say something wrong?

Did we ask them to give us stuff?

Hey, I try to remind myself that it won't always be like this. After all, old Hunk and I struggled a bit when we were young, too. But we finally broke away.

And now, look at where we are!

In only a few years, our remaining two children – both boys – will be leaving the nest. Yes, we can wait, but we do look forward to that big day.

Old Hunk and I will have this big old house all to ourselves. I'll have a sewing room and he'll have an office. I'll be able to talk on the phone any time I want to, and he'll know where all his tools are.

Will we be lonely? Nah, we'll manage.

Besides, I'm sure we'll still have our oldest son's dog.

15
MMQ:
On The Naming of Cars

One summer's day, Rascal and Girlfriend were visiting when my husband and I brought home the latest addition to our family. We all gathered around the new arrival and admired him.

"He looks just like Fred," Rascal announced.

Oh no, not Fred!

In the past, I'd made fun of Fred (behind his back of course). Could it be payback time?

"Nah, Fred has more rust," I countered, and everyone agreed, even Rascal. (Whew!) After all, Fred spends months out in the rain, with nothing – not even a tarp – to shelter him from the elements.

Did I mention that Fred is a truck?

Fred belongs to our friend, Mr. Fixit, who visits us sometimes. Usually, Fred is saddled up with all kinds of useful stuff like shovels, chain saws, paint brushes, and ladders. And all kinds of debris, such as tree limbs, McDonald's drink cups, empty paint cans, three-legged chairs, and bags of outgrown clothes.

(Yep. Fred's new car smell didn't last long.)

You see, Fred is a work horse.

Which brings me to my point: Why do so many Americans name their vehicles?

I think I know. It's because, subconsciously, we wish we still rode horses.

After all, horses are nice creatures. When we talk to them, they perk up their ears and listen. If we sit on them, we can feel the warmth of their bodies under our legs.

A person can build a relationship with a horse, and that's why many of us still want to build relationships with our cars.

(Or at least we try. You know – it depends upon the beast. Some cars are just more docile than others.)

When I brought home my new-old truck, Rascal's girlfriend scored some major points with our family. Not only did she admire our rusty, dented, sixteen-year-old Chevy LUV pick-up and easily see past his battle scars to all his strong points, but also she helped to name him and attended the christening.

After we'd established that Mr. Fixit's Fred had more rust than our new-old truck, Girlfriend came waltzing over (girls who are in LUV always waltz – have you noticed?) and helped to inspect the old dobbin.

She commented on how solid his bed was, and agreed that a good sanding and a coat of primer would easily solve the rust problem. After all, the rust hadn't eaten through the floor yet.

(Here, the aging vehicle began to whinny in gleeful acknowledgement.)

And wasn't it great that he had a long bed?

(He pawed the ground at this. Oh, he was a smart one!)

A long bed would be oh-so-useful, she said. We all nodded.

(I could see visions of transporting furniture to a honeymoon cottage were galloping through Girlfriend's head. When was Rascal going to propose?)

Girlfriend nodded with approval at the almost-new, black-walled tires, then gasped in admiration at the four petite cylinders and that darling old-fashioned thing called a carburetor.

(This time, the old truck fairly neighed!)

Pricey computerized fuel injection? No way! Here was some tack we could fiddle with and keep running, all on our own.

Visions of my high school Auto Shop class cantered through my head, and I felt pangs of greasy engine love brewing in my system. I patted the old truck's sides.

"Good boy," I whispered. Then to Girlfriend, "Help me name him," I urged.

Girlfriend was misty-eyed for a minute and gazed off into space. Then she brightened.

"How about Billy Bob?"

I was impressed. She felt a real kinship that truck (probably since she was hoping to become a member of the family sometime soon, herself).

Billy Bob. It suited him perfectly.

It was the first time I'd ever owned a male vehicle, and it took some getting used to. Up

"Hi ho, Billy Bob . . . awaaay!"

until that day, all of the cars I'd ever owned had been either female or unisex.

(And yeah, some of them were real mules).

My first car, a 1939 Nash, was the most female of them all – Passionella. I invested in her all I'd earned during an entire summer spent packing pears in the high desert, in between my sophomore and junior years of high school.

However, ours was a short but beautiful relationship. For as it turned out, Pashy was ailing and unbeknownst to me, was on her last legs. After she sat for one full semester, half dismantled in the Auto Shop parking lot, I finally had to shoot her and send her to the great clover fields in the sky.

(May she rust in peace.)

Then there was Josephine, My Flying Machine, a gray 1949 Plymouth, complete with purple sun visor and original upholstery. Josephine and I were the same age – seventeen – when I purchased her for $200 from a neighbor, after a second summer packing pears. Josephine was a trotter, a pretty little filly who loved to go anywhere, anytime. For my eighteenth birthday, I gave Josey new seat covers, and for graduation, four new tires. In return, Josey never bucked, never spooked, and always put her best foot forward.

You know pardner, sometimes it's a hard life out on the range, but if you got you a faithful vehicle, you'll always make it back home to the stables. Yee-ha!

Well, old Billy Bob has proven

to be a fine steed, indeed. Imagine my delight when a friend offered me twice what I paid for him only a month after I'd purchased him.

"No thanks," I told him. After all, Billy is not just any old truck. He's a member of the family.

Besides, Rascal and the future Mrs. Huckstep are gonna get hitched real soon, and it'll be kinda handy to have a spare set of hooves around the old homestead.

But for now, it's time to ride off into the sunset, *Kimosabe*.

"Hi ho, Billy Bob . . . awaaay!"

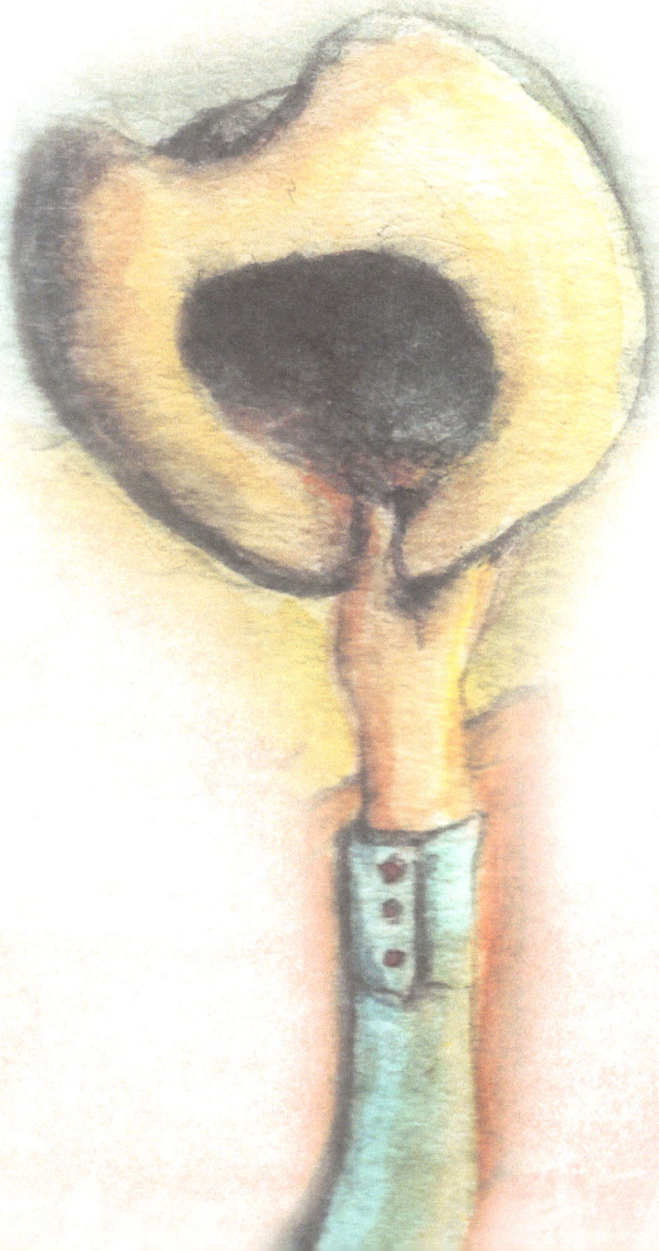

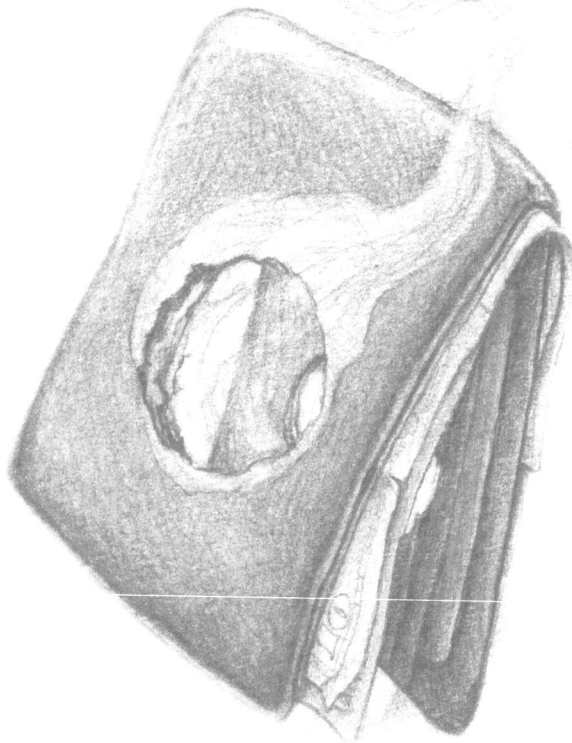

16
MMQ: On May Day

<A>ttention anybody who has a relative.

Would that be you?

Got a son, daughter, mother, father, husband, wife, brother, sister, grandma, grandpa, aunt, uncle or cousin? What about an in-law, out-law, or half-step version of any of the above?

(Or how about an a-version?)

And don't you forget about extended family. These would be your friends, neighbors,

sweethearts, colleagues, and fiancées.

Uh-huh, I thought so. You got some.

Now listen carefully to what I have to tell you, for your very life may depend upon it. This is a public service announcement for anyone who knows anybody at all: Watch your backs folks, cuz there's a mean *hombre* ridin' into town, and as surely as Monday follows Sunday, he's a comin'.

Look out ladies and gents, cuz the May Day Bandit's hot on your trail. He's got both barrels loaded, and he's gonna hunt you down like a varmint, line you up in his sights, and squeeze the trigger.

Boom!

He's gonna blast a hole in you the size of Missouri, right between your wallet and your bank account, if you don't run for cover quick.

In fact, it may already be too late!

Just when you thought it was safe to look at your checkbook balance again (a whole five months after Christmas), suddenly it's May Day, opening day of the season of celebrations. I guarantee you that very soon, somebody you know, somewhere on this planet, is gonna ask you to celebrate something of importance with them.

(Read, "Send money.")

So, why don't I hear any celebrating out there?

When I was a girl, I used to celebrate the first day of May and it didn't cost me a cent. I even looked forward to it – my springtime celebration of life.

I'd decorate a newspaper with crayons, roll it into a cone shape, staple it together, and add a handle to make a basket. Then I'd wander all around the yard and pick flowers – dandelions, geraniums, wild flowers, weeds, you name it.

I'd fill up my paper basket with blooms, sneak over to a neighbor's house, loop the basket handle over the doorknob, ring the doorbell, and run away. Then I'd watch from a hiding spot and snigger when the door opened and the neighbors found my anonymous, *free* May Day gift.

It was fun.

I gave flower baskets to every family on the block and especially loved leaving flowers for people I didn't even know. Why? Because they couldn't thank me and I took joy, purely in the giving.

After all, it was May Day, and in my heart I was Queen of the May.

Boy, was I naïve – celebrating life for free?

If only I'd known what the future held, I wouldn't have been so bloomin' happy!

For nowadays, May Day holds a special terror all its own. It's the pay-up-or-die day, and survival is the name of the game.

It starts in the mail on May 1st, when everyone you've ever known or said hello to suddenly sends you cards. They're the kind of cards that take three envelopes, fancy tissue paper, and several first, middle, and last names, just to say, "You owe me, sucker, and you'd better pay up, big. Fork over some cash, now."

Bang!

You've got yer high school grads, yer college grads, yer grad-school grads, and yer end-of-the-fiscal-year retirees.

("Ahhh! Ya got me pardner!")

Before you know it, you've got yer Mother's Day gifts, yer Mother's Day brunches, yer Father's Day gifts, and yer Father's Day all-you-can-eat buffets.

Kerpow!

("I'm hit! I'm hit!")

Then you've got yer prom tickets, yer prom dresses, yer prom tux, and yer limo rentals.

("Owwww! I'm uh dyin' here.")

Then, just when yer staggerin' and ya cain't hardly stand on yer own two feet no more, here come those bridal showers, weddings, wedding clothes, and vacation plans.

("Oooh, I'm a gonner!")

Next thing you know, it's the Fourth of July and you're lying on the ground, feet pointing straight up at God Almighty, and you're beggin' your Maker, "Please God, please just let me die."

You've poured out so much blood, you've had to go for three refills at the local blood bank, just to keep on bleedin'.

But don't ya know, you're not allowed to die?

That's the worst part of it all. It's called "The Curse of the May Day Bandit," *cuz nobody ever gets to die.* No sirree, cuz

"I'm hit! I'm hit!"

ya cain't get blood outta a dead man's wallet!

(Nope, that's the government's job.)

So you've just gotta keep on givin' till the season of celebration comes to its natural end, somewhere around the start of the school year.

Now, I know what some of you are thinking. Cuz all of this fussin' and carryin' on is making some of you feel mighty guilty. (Of course you *are* guilty, and you *should* feel that way!)

You're the ones who sent out all those announcements and had the audacity to do something important like graduate from high school, get married, give birth, or retire from the workforce.

But couldn't you have just kept quiet about it?

Why does everybody have to be so doggone noisy about things? Why can't we all just go quietly about our business and never bother anybody else?

"Shhh, we're getting married next week, but it's a secret. Don't say a word."

I tried suggesting this to Rascal recently, but he and his fiancée just wouldn't go for it. (Who raised that boy?) So I find myself in a most embarrassing position.

I confess! I gave Rascal's fiancée a list of names and addresses for their wedding announcements. And I want you to know that I feel like a lowdown, good for nothin' sidewinder.

(But hey, I've been writing checks for other people's children for decades, so it's not like I haven't earned the right to dip into the pot some, myself. Right?)

So if you get a wedding announcement from my family, I just want to tell you, "I feel your pain."

And to those of you who've already sent me your announcements, I say, "The check's in the mail, so wait for it."

(May Day! May Day! May Day!)

17
MMQ: On Being Poked In The Eye

I'll always remember seventh grade Homeroom, and my personal twelve minutes of daily hell. And Paunchy Puberty Boy who sat next to me, never speaking.

He spent the entire ten minutes – between the flag salute and the dismissal bell – drawing grotesquely bloody eyeballs, with various sharp objects skewered into them: Knives, javelins, shards of glass, and his personal favorite – long-tyned forks.

It was the forks that always sent shivers down my spine.

And the forks that floated up to memory, decades later, when I awoke from eye surgery, feeling as if my left eye had suddenly become the grisly object of one of Puberty Boy's creations.

"Better than a poke in the eye with a sharp stick," another memory floated up from the hollows of my brain.

"Yeah? Well, try a long-tyned fork next time and see how that works for ya!" I shot back.

Or thought I shot back.

I was waking up from the anesthetic with the growing realization that the doctors had played an ugly trick on me. Instead of re-attaching my retina, they had forked my eyeball!

Paunchy Puberty Boy had grown up to become an ophthalmic surgeon and had stalked me down for the forking!

"Get me outta here!" I shouted, but strong arms held me down and muffled my speech with an oxygen mask. And then I heard

a pathetic voice whimper, "My eye hurts," and I realized that the pathetic voice was mine.

Puberty Boy had finished his dirty work, and all that remained was for me to die in agony – like a butterfly, netted and pinned down to a cork board.

Fifteen minutes later, and with twenty milliliters of something very potent coursing through my veins, I was wheeled back to the ward, snoring.

Oh my eye still hurt, but I was resigned to my fate. My eye had been forked. And royally, too.

The next morning, a cheerful nurse unwrapped my eyeball and examined it. "It looks good!" she gushed, perhaps a little too gushily, and my antennae began to go up.

"Alright if I go to the ladies room?" I asked.

Yes, and since I was steady on my feet, she let me tinkle on my own. I peered in the mirror and that's when I saw it – the remains of what once had been a rather cute little eyeball.

Paunchy Puberty Boy had grown up to become an ophthalmic surgeon
and had stalked me down for the forking!

Actually, I couldn't even see my eyeball.

Resting on my left cheek like a flabby, fleshy inner-tube, my left eyelid was inflated to ten times its normal size, in both length and width. The lashes spread out across my cheek like a second mouth that smirked back at me, and suddenly I realized that my face looked rather familiar.

"Quasimodo?"

Quasimodo.

Staring out from the mirror was a hideously contorted face, a face that only a gypsy girl full of pity could love. Puberty Boy had extracted his revenge, and overnight, I had been transformed into The Hunchback of Notre Dame.

My friend Fiona came to collect me after lunch. "You look dreadful!" she opined and gave me a hug.

Then I remembered that Fiona was part gypsy and I thanked God I'd chosen her for the drive home. She seated me at my kitchen table, made clucking noises, fixed me a sandwich, picked up a tambourine and danced a bit, then whirled out the door, her mission of mercy at an end.

I wallowed on the sofa for days, married to pain and oozing goo from my speared eye. Drifting in and out of a stupor and watching fifty-year-old movies on TV with my un-speared eye.

Feeling like a slug and looking like a moron.

Some people call it healing.

I call it suffering.

On the fifth day I gingerly took a shower and began to feel somewhat human. My eyelid had retreated from my cheek and now protruded from above my eye like a miniature bagel. It was still puffy, but at least now I could see my eyeball.

Ugh. Paunchy Puberty Boy was right.

Skewered eyeballs are red and grossly squished out of shape. How I wished I could pull down my eyelid like a window shade and block out that hideous sight.

Sight? Sight!? Did somebody mention SIGHT!?? Yes, I mentioned it, but I seem to have been the only one who did.

"Hello? Hello! When am I supposed to regain my sight, thank you very much?"

"Come back and see the good doctor in four weeks and we'll talk about it then."

And with those words, it became official: I was – literally and figuratively – stuck in the dark.

On the ninth day, I was watching TV with my good eye, when a thin layer of sight gradually appeared in my – for lack of a better word – bad eye.

(Bad eye! Bad, bad eye!)

At the top of my field of vision I could barely discern the mirror which hung over the fireplace in our living room.

But under the fireplace, my vision was occluded by what looked like a big pool of dark water, which moved and sloshed whenever I moved my head – which was a lot because I sat there for over an hour, fascinated, my film forgotten. Covering up my good eye and giving my bad eye a chance to redeem itself.

Hmmmm. Was this what they called "seeing?" Would I have to spend the rest of my days peering at life as if I were looking through the porthole of a surfacing submarine?

A frantic call to the ward assured me that my full field of vision would return, in degrees, from the top down. I just had to wait for it. Wait – and watch.

It would have been really nice if they had told me that before they forked my eyeball.

But come to think of it, I can't remember Paunchy Puberty Boy saying even one word, in ten months of Homeroom. All he ever did was draw, and grin, and look at me as if he had plans . . . .

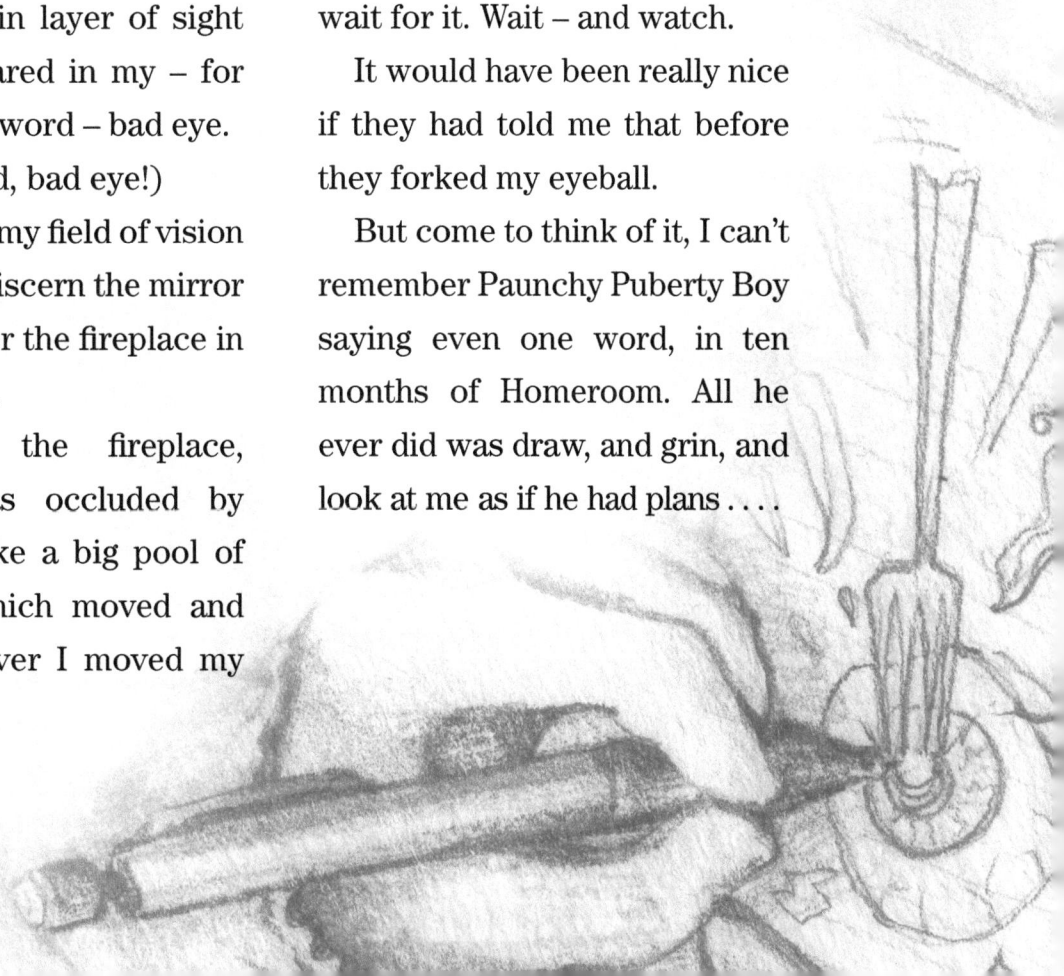

18
MMQ:
On Bedtime Crimes

What is it about the approach of bedtime that can turn an angelic little four-year-old into a master criminal, whose nightly shootouts and subversive activities could undermine the entire state of Texas?

When my four-year-old grandson stayed with us over the holidays, my husband and I got to see a true master criminal in action. Each night, promptly at 8:00 p.m. (or 8:47, or 9:22, or whenever his bedraggled mother suddenly realized it was waaaay past his bedtime), his mom (our daughter) would announce, "It's time for bed."

This would elicit his prompt reply, "I'm hungry."

And then the fun would begin.

If Mom's answer to his statement were, "I told you at dinner that you had to eat everything because there would be no snacks later on," then he would simply repeat his statement.

"But I'm hungry."

On the other hand, if Mom ignored his remarks and, instead, employed his tactic by repeating her words, "It's time for bed," then he would launch an all-out attack and holler –

"I . . . AM . . . HUNGREEEEEEEEEEEE!"

And broadcast to the entire state of California an update on the contents of his stomach, or the lack thereof.

That boom that shook California at 8:08 on the night of December 22nd was not an earthquake. No. It was the rebel yell of the Killer Rugrat.

Next, Killer would launch a second offensive: weeping, wailing, and gnashing of teeth. But if this did not produce Mom's immediate surrender, it was then that my grandson's true genius for crime became apparent. For we could never predict his next move.

Therefore, Killer always retained the element of surprise.

One night he ran down the hallway screaming, darted into his room, slammed the door behind him and careened straight onto his bed. We could hear the springs reverberating, way back in the living room.

I whispered, "What if I run in there, turn off the lights, lock the door, then dash back and turn the TV up loud, 'till he stops screaming?"

I grew giddy with the sense of victory. I thought we had won.

But before my daughter could answer, the bedroom door opened and out my little grandson emerged, fuming.

He stood there, eyes hard as steel, fists curled up into cannon

balls, primed and ready to explode. Then suddenly he was coughing, gagging, turning red in the face. He fell to the floor, gasping for breath.

My daughter raced over and crouched at his side.

He stared up into her eyes, opened his mouth, and struggled to draw in one long, asthmatic breath. Then a word formed on his chubby little lips, and he managed a pitiful whisper.

"Med . . . i . . . cine?"

Mom raced to the kitchen, grabbed a small brown bottle, dashed back to her son, sat at his side, poured red liquid into a spoon and then into his mouth, then cradled his head in her lap.

He closed his eyes.

She stroked his hair for a bit, then his eyelids fluttered open and he said ever-so-sweetly, "Could I have a drink of milk to wash away the taste of medicine?"

And as she busied herself in the kitchen, we heard the final terms of his peace-offering: "And some bread and butter, too?"

Minutes later, Killer sat in the kitchen, the sweet taste of victory melting in his mouth like . . . well, like butter. Beaten, old Hunk and I sat in the living room and sniveled. We had become victims – yet again – of juvenile fraud.

This is the way that the parenting ends, not with a bang, but with a whimper.

Interesting. The next night Mom went over to a girlfriend's house, and Killer's dad had to put the little delinquent to bed. But when Dad said, "It's time for bed," that child did the most amazing things.

He put away his toys, got into his pajamas, and climbed into bed.

Hello?!

Now, I've been thinking about this for weeks, and I believe I've finally discovered the real reason why children obey their dads and do not obey their moms. It has nothing to do with who suffers through labor pains, or who walks the halls at night when they have the flu, or who

The sweet taste of victory melted in his mouth like . . .
well, like butter.

usually puts them to bed each night, or who usually disciplines them, or who doesn't.

No.

All that is just a load of hooey from a lot of nincompoops.

Nope.

The real reason that children can manipulate their mothers and cannot manipulate their dads is because children know all their mothers' fears. This means that they know all the buttons they need to push, to make their mamas jump.

Now, how do they know their mothers' fears?

Simple. Mothers tell them.

"Eat your dinner or you'll be hungry later on."

(Mama Button: She's afraid I'll starve.)

"An apple a day keeps the doctor away."

(Mama Button: She's afraid I'll get sick.)

"Look both ways, or you'll get run over."

(Mama Button: She's afraid I'll have an accident.)

You catch my drift, folks?

So moms, I have finally discovered how you can fight back against the nightly bedtime crimes and win. Do what I did, and my mother, and my mother's mother before me. Run, don't walk, to the nearest stranger – any stranger – and grab the first one you see.

Ask *him* to put your kids to bed. Since your kids will be un-acquainted with his fears (claustrophobia, arachnophobia, hydrophobia, whatever!), he is bound to succeed where you have failed.

It's as simple as that!

But you must do this *yesterday*.

After all, you don't want to end up raising the next Billy the Kid, now do you?!

19
MMQ:
On Life in the Country

After I received my B.A., I knew I still lacked life experience, but I did not know which kind.

(And no, I wasn't looking for my M.R.S.)

So I decided to fly to Scotland and visit some friends across the ocean, and it was there that I set out to "find myself."

My search didn't take long.

Obviously, I needed to get to know the earth upon which I depended, if ever I were to understand life!

I had sixteen years of schooling, yet I couldn't distinguish a potato plant from a pea plant, to save my soul. Well, if it were harvest time and the plants had big potatoes or miniature peas growing on them, then I might know the difference. (Duh!)

Oh, I could distinguish between a gerund and a participial, all right, but that didn't amount to a hill of beans (if beans grew in hills, which, quite frankly, I did not know). I had to admit it: In the basic elements of survival, I was a moron – and it was time for my real education to begin.

So I moved in to a 500 year-old country cottage.

It had no electricity, no gas, no shower, and no neighbors.

(Well, the rent was cheap.)

But it did have a steady supply of wood from a nearby sawmill. It also had an open fireplace whose draft could be diverted sideways to a cast-iron stove, which heated a small cooking surface and a tiny oven. Brilliant!

Best of all – the cottage had evidence of past gardening glory, for there were fifteen overgrown currant bushes, ten straggly gooseberry bushes, and some weedy plots where garden beds had once flourished.

I had struck survival gold.

My friends helped me move in, then headed back to the city. I felt sorry for them, and suddenly rather superior. After all, I was about to find myself and they were still lost.

Alone in paradise, I decided to go for a walk. I trekked half a mile along a sheep trail that traversed the pasture where my new home was situated. Then I sat down on a rock wall and closed my eyes to commune with nature.

Wait . . . what was that? And that – and that – and that!?

It was growing difficult for me to concentrate. Cuz it was just a little too noisy out there!

"Baaaaa. Mmmooooh! Buzzzzz. Tweet tweet!"

My gosh, what a racket. Didn't they have any parks around there? Where, in this vast countryside, could a person go to get some peace?

Back at the cottage, it was

getting chilly so I decided to light a fire.

(I can do this.)

I sawed some wood, chopped some kindling (ouch!), then built a fire – just like the one I'd seen Spin and Marty build on "The Mickey Mouse Club" television show when I was a kid. Then I touched a match to the paper and the flame enlarged, flared, fizzled and died out. (Wah!)

I tried again, same thing. (Wah again!)

I really wanted to do this. The kindling was turning black, all right, but it just wouldn't catch fire.

Maybe I was making the wrong shape with the kindling? Maybe it wasn't supposed to be arranged like a teepee?

(Gee, it worked for Spin and Marty.)

I persisted for thirty more minutes, failed miserably, then gave up. I would never trust another TV tip again. (Soooo Mickey Mouse.)

I lit a candle, ate a peanut butter sandwich for dinner, shivered in the cold for a bit, then climbed into my sleeping bag and fell asleep.

No, a crowing rooster did not wake me up the next morning. A bleating ewe did.

It was spring and she was in labor – right outside my sitting room window. (Gosh!) Shivering in the cold and damp, I fixed myself another peanut butter sandwich, pulled on my jacket, and perched on the window sill to watch the birth.

(Without electricity, morning cartoons were definitely out.)

Weird. That ewe did everything the Lamaze books said to do. She panted just like a human mama in a sterile delivery room. Then in between contractions, that ewe closed her eyes and relaxed. A few minutes later, she started panting again.

And so it went until eventually she pushed, stood up and took a few steps – just as her baby slid out, wrapped up in a filmy package. Then she turned around and licked him to life, until he was clean and wriggling.

Minutes later his twin was born, and she licked him to life, too. All finished, she closed her eyes and took a nap.

(Just like that – no worries!)

Wow, giving birth didn't look so difficult, from where I sat. As a matter of fact, it looked rather marvelous.

(But I had to wonder . . . where do you suppose that ewe learned to read? And who gave her a copy of that Lamaze book, anyway?)

An hour later, the farmer arrived to administer antibiotics to the new mom. He was a wiry fellow in overalls, who finished his work efficiently, then turned to go. This was my golden opportunity!

I bolted out the front door and ran after him, hollering. I'd forgotten that I'd slept in my clothes, but as soon as I saw the look on his face, I remembered.

"Hi. I'm a moron and I don't know how to light a fire," I jabbered. "And I slept in my clothes last night, so I look like a moron, too."

(It wasn't the best of introductions, but it did the trick.)

The farmer nodded briefly, then volunteered to show me how to "lay the fire."

I took him inside, where he knelt down on the hearth and looked up the chimney. "You'll be needing the flue open."

(Wow. Good idea!)

He pulled a soot-encrusted lever.

"And you must lay the sticks like a checkerboard – just so. They'll rest on one another after the paper's burnt, and the fire will have something tae gnaw on."

In 90 seconds he built a three-layered fire, with paper doughnuts on the bottom, covered by a grid of kindling, and topped by criss-crossed hunks of wood. He touched a match to

"Hi. I'm a moron and I don't know how to light a fire."

one corner, and the whole thing flared, sucked air, then crackled with life.

I took notes. I drew diagrams. I grew excited. I could do this!

"There's a copper boiler at the back of the fire, and in an hour there'll be hot water for your bath. Cheerio!"

He avoided my eyes and fled from the room.

These country farmers. So shy.

But hey, one day into my survival education, and already I'd learned how to "lay the fire." And soon, I'd be soaking in a nice, hot bath. Oh, life was good.

An hour later when I ran my bath water, I glanced in the mirror and saw a bizarre-looking creature. Me!

Soot marks streaked across my face from ear to ear, and black fingerprints dotted my forehead like spots on a leopard. I looked like a confused Indian on the war path.

I bared my teeth – and saw that soot had also blackened one of my front incisors.

No wonder the good farmer had fled.

Okay, so I was a moron.

Hey, I'd already known that before I moved in. But today I was less of a moron than I had been, yesterday. And tomorrow? Well, tomorrow was another day! (Yea, Scarlett.)

"You can do this!" I told the wacky Indian in the mirror. And then I washed off all the evidence and came clean.

20
MMQ:
On The Truth About
Boys and Girls

When my sons were born, it was considered progressive for boys to play with dolls. So I bought baby dolls for the little darlings and did my best to encourage their mothering instincts.

Of course, I probably confused them, too, since they could not actually become mothers – anatomically speaking, that is.

But I knew that one day their wives would rise up and call me blessed because I had trained their future husbands to be nurturers of baby dolls.

(Gee, it sounded good, back then.)

And since I was a pacifist at the time, I did not allow my sons to play with war toys of any kind – neither toy guns, nor tanks, nor missiles, nor dynamite, nor napalm, nor nuclear warheads. *Nada. El zippo.* None of the above.

(Basically, they just couldn't have any fun.)

But a curious thing happened.

We lived on an isolated farm cottage and had no TV or other outside influences. Where then, did my sons learn to play war games?

(From their hormones, maybe?)

For by the time they had reached the age of three, sticks were guns and knives, any toy with wheels was a tank, and anything that would explode when thrown – like a dirt clod or an orange – was a bomb.

And they positively worshipped our nearest neighbor, Cave Man,

who lived just a mile down the road. Why? Because each spring, their beloved Cave would kill half the rooks that lived in the beech trees which surrounded our cottage.

The farmer (our landlord) commissioned him to shoot down these predatory birds each year – to keep nature in balance, or so he claimed. And this became one of the high points of my boys' kid year.

It ranked right up there with Christmas and birthday parties – the Annual Rook Massacre.

"Hooray! Cave Man's here!" a tiny voice would sing out, and then two little boys would scramble to take up their positions on the fence, where they would remain for hours.

They studied Cave's every move and gazed with loving admiration, each time a shot rang out and a large black bird would plummet forty feet to the grass below.

UGH. That killer instinct.

How many mothers have despaired over the presence of such a force in their male child? How could it be, that inside the chest of each cherubic little boy there beats the heart of an assassin?

I don't have the answer to that question. Sorry!

(You'll have to ask the sexperts on that one.)

But I do have more observations.

A couple of years after the Cave Man era, I was single again and shared a big house with a young couple and their daughter, the Drama Queen. Queenie was five and loved to play dollies (unlike my little assassins).

One morning, Queenie and her friend, Cutie Pie, spent hours fussing over their dollies and parading them around the living room in baby buggies. The little mothers had just retired to the kitchen to have a tea party, when my older son and his friend stampeded in from the back yard (where they had been shooting bad guys, no doubt), then made tracks for the living room.

Sonny and Friend spotted the baby buggies and knew instantly what to do. They said not a word, but went straight to their work, Sonny behind one buggy and Friend behind the other.

Rrrrramming speed . . . keeerash!

It was Baby Buggy Demolition Derby, as Sonny and Friend

They said not a word but went straight to their work.

smashed those buggies together like charging bulls (which they were, actually).

Queenie and Cutie came racing out of the kitchen, hollering. Soon, they were pouring tears and tender words over their baby dolls, and hurling insults and accusations at those bad! bad! bulls who had ceased charging (wisely) and were now cowering.

And that's when the light of understanding began to dawn.

Here it is – the truth about boys and girls.

(Drum roll, please!)

Girls are born to nurture, while boys are born to fight and defend.

It's unmistakable.

Don't ask me why! (I'll leave that to the sexperts, too.)

But even Libby, my gal-pal who burned her bra in the 60's, has worn overalls for thirty years, and is a card-carrying member of NOW, has come full circle. She raised two boys and a girl, and doggone it if she didn't discover that there is a difference!

She gave baby dolls to her boys. They shaved the dolls' heads and turned them into war victims.

She gave her daughter a cap gun and caps. Her daughter abandoned the gun, took the caps, and popped them on the sidewalk with a rock. (It was too much trouble to load the gun.) Go figure!

I am aware that my amazing discoveries will be hotly contested in some arenas. And I apologize if I have offended anyone, anywhere, for any reason.

(I'm not standing too close to you, am I?)

To any women whose sensitivities I have wounded, I say, "Write me a long letter and tell me how this makes you feel."

To the men whom I might have offended, I say, "My daddy can beat up your daddy. So deal with it!"

21
MMQ:
On Selling a House

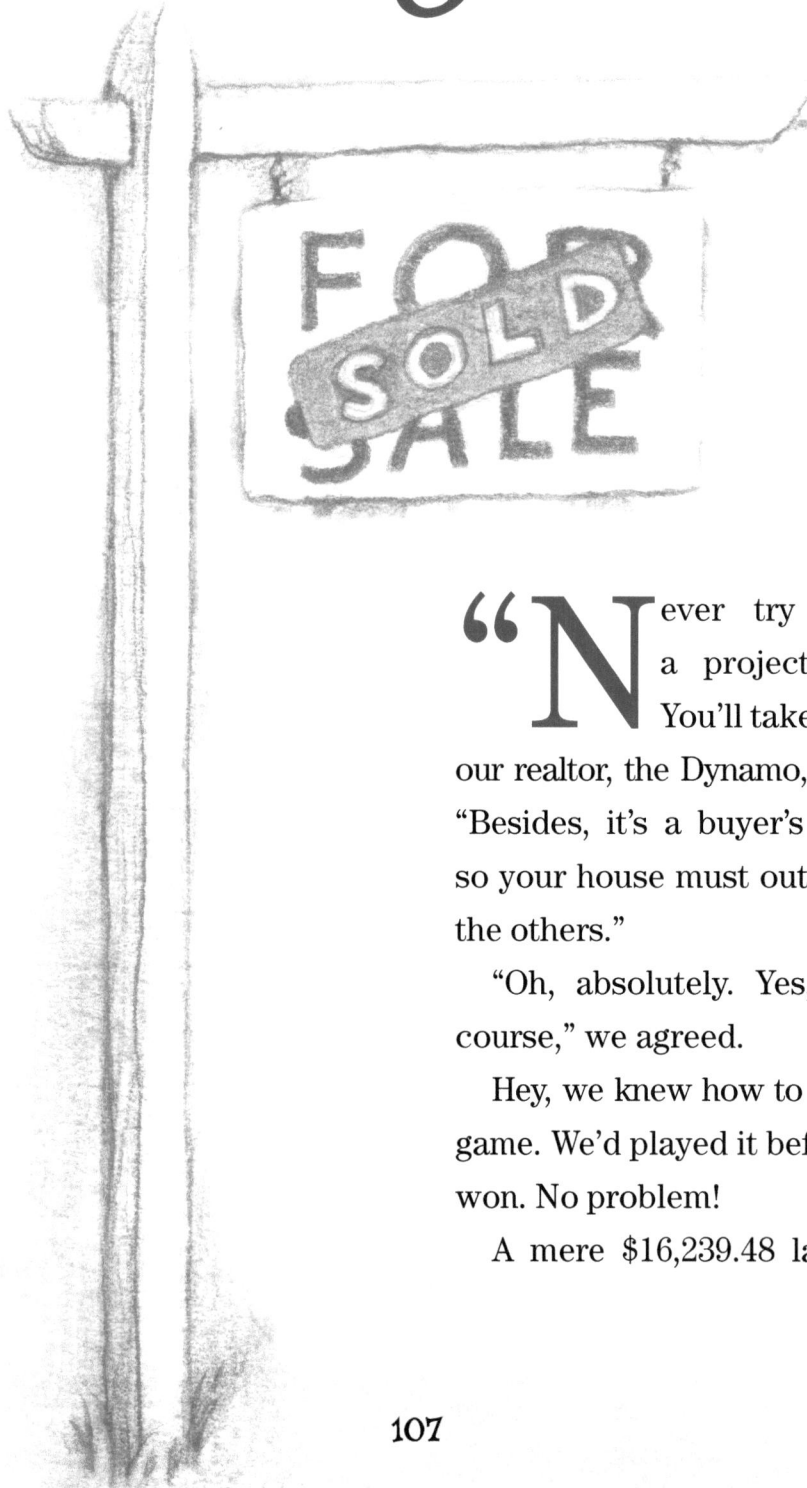

"Never try to sell a project house. You'll take a bath," our realtor, the Dynamo, warned. "Besides, it's a buyer's market, so your house must outshine all the others."

"Oh, absolutely. Yes, yes of course," we agreed.

Hey, we knew how to play this game. We'd played it before, and won. No problem!

A mere $16,239.48 later, our

"no-longer-a-project house" was ready.

Or so we thought.

For two months, a never-ending parade of tradesmen had traipsed through our peaceful home like an army on maneuvers – ripping some things out, putting other things back in, painting anything that would not move, and updating everything that did.

Lighting, flooring, sprinkling, cooling, heating, dining, drooling, and even coping mechanisms – all were made to "outshine" the competition. Then we paid a neighborhood kid to vacuum all three floors, while we polished everything from roof to basement, both inside and out – and finally phoned up the Dynamo.

"We're ready!" we told him and exhaled a unified sigh of relief.

Nothing remained but to sit back and wait for the buyers.

Wrong!

The next day, Dynamo and his bride, Dynamite, descended on our happy home like a plague of Valkeries, complete with Wagnerian arias, Viking helmets, and a truck full of lugubrious furnishings that would make even Count Dracula fly into a panic.

"This is very trendy right now," Mrs. D smiled, then deftly removed my colorful throw pillows and substituted her own specially-reserved-for-staging-the-sale throw pillows.

Big black leather ones, they were, with ugly brass studs.

Perfect for entertaining vampires.

"Let's move the furniture so the room looks bigger," Mr. D enthused.

Then D and D sprang into action. And before I knew it, the cozy conversation area in our living room disappeared, and all our overstuffed furniture lay strung out along the walls like a fleet of fishing boats . . . just close enough to one another to flash signals, in case of emergency.

Well, the room did look bigger. Heck, now you could even roller skate in front of the fireplace.

Who needed to talk?

"I never use throw rugs," Mrs. D advised, as she squatted on the floor and rolled up the flowery Persian carpet I'd inherited from my mother. Ten seconds later, a rainbow of color disappeared into a cigar-shaped tube, and Mr. D catapulted it up onto the top shelf of the garage – out of sight, but definitely not out of mind.

And speaking of minds – I was about to lose mine!

"I'm sorry," I protested, "but I draw the line at putting guillotines and escutcheons in my kitchen."

When my back had been turned – out in the garage, watching flying carpets, no doubt – Dynamite had climbed up onto my kitchen counter, stood up and reached way up high, then placed a long row of seedy objects along the shelf on the top of my cabinets.

I shivered. Distinct memories began to float back to me, memories of the medieval prison I'd toured years ago, while visiting London. Any moment, I expected a foul, gap-toothed guard to appear out of nowhere, wrestle me to the floor, and clap leg irons onto my ankles.

What was up with all these trendy furnishings?

Sheesh! Just how depressed was this up-and-coming generation – the people who were most likely to purchase our happy home? Any more of their furnishings, and we'd want to burn the place to the ground, dance in the ashes, and prowl around the neighborhood in search of spiders to munch on.

Cuckoo!

I decided to put my foot down.

"These drapes will need to be ironed," the Dynamo announced, then thrust a package of wrinkled, floor-to-ceiling drapery panels into my hands. I'd made the mistake of purchasing them

Just how depressed was this up-and-coming generation –
the people who were most likely to purchase our happy home?

a few years back, when some trendy linen store had gone out of business. Too busy to put the drapes up, I'd been happy to let the package gather dust in a corner of our bedroom – until now.

"They'll make the master bedroom look larger," Mrs. D's head appeared behind her cohort's. She crinkled her eyes in what I'm sure was meant to be a sign of friendship.

Larger. Right. Larger was good – I knew that. But ironing anything at all was strictly against my religion. Years ago, I had given it all up for Lent and had never re-Lented.

I said three Hail Mary's and four Our Fathers, then got out the ironing board.

Dutifully, I slaved away in the basement for the next hour, while mysterious sounds filtered down to me from regions overhead. What were they doing up there?

Old Hunk had dashed off to town on some fraudulent errand and here I was, locked in the house, alone with the dastardly Dynamos.

Creepy.

Mr. D descended to the nether-regions, snorted at me in feigned compassion, then helped bring the newly-ironed panels back upstairs.

That's when I saw it. A gargantuan, black iron mirror now perched above our bed like an executioner, hovering over the place where we, the sacrificial couple, must lay our necks and prepare to meet our Maker.

Ugh.

"It makes the room look larger" the two D's chorused, as I ran out of the room, screaming. How could I sleep in there?

"Just don't look at it," Dynamite trotted after me and pressed her cheek to mine.

Then she dusted off her hands in triumph. Her work here was done.

"Don't even think about the furnishings," the Dynamo gushed, as he too gave me a hug. "Think about all the money you're going to make."

Then he pounded his For Sale sign into the front yard and disappeared.

As they drove off into the night, I'm sure I saw a dark blue curtain close in around their van, followed by the sound of thunderous applause. The Wagnerian opera had come to an end. And finally, I could relax.

But not in our house.

Hunk and I checked into a hotel within the hour – the most colorful one we could find.

All our lives, we've avoided pink flamingos, yellow duckies, and heart-shaped beds. But that night we found them oddly comforting.

And let the buying begin!

BONUS CHAPTER
MMQ:
On Bridal Showers

N eed a recipe to take to a bridal shower? Here's a popular dish from the Huckstep family cookbook. It's a tasty little entrée I cooked up for Sonny and his fiancée.

Recipe For A Happy Home

Take one spring chicken with a good, healthy heart,
salt him carefully with an ounce of prevention,
then marinate him in a whole pound of cure.
(He'll need it.)
Introduce to a second spring chicken with a second healthy heart.
She should be equally salted and adequately marinated.
(But use good judgment –
some chickens require less cure than others.)

Stir both together with fun,
sweeten with humor,
dust with romance,
then cover with a mantle of friendship
and leave in a safe place for months
to ferment.
Next, punch down with disappointment
and knead with adversity
until the skins are no longer thin
and the flavor no longer sticky sweet.
Then, working quickly,
add a dash of joy,
baste with honorable intent, and
circle with a ring of unconditional love.

Dress well, brush with the oil of gladness, then bind
together forever with vows of commitment.

Cover again,
protect from drafts,
and leave for several more months
until nearly doubled in volume.
Then, when the big day finally arrives –
dress well
brush with the oil of gladness
and bind together forever with vows of commitment,
adding in a generous scoop of witnesses.
(Correct seasoning, using humor and romance, to taste.)

Sizzle in a tropical paradise for seven days,
then soak in patience and forgiveness for decades
and bake in a moderate oven
for a lifetime.

Coming Soon!

2015

(But if we're being realistic, let's make that 2016.)

MARY MARY QUITE

On Grandma Gold
(And Other Anti-Aging Supplements)

2016

(And just who are we kidding? Make that 2017!)

MARY MARY QUITE

On Life In The 21st Century
(And Other Anti-Social Behaviors)